Tribalism to Modernity

Terry & Maggie Sharp

Tribal
Roles People Play Today

ISBN 9781091498044

Tribalism to Modernity

Dedicated to my partner Maggie her support to this project and friends and neighbours who gave me the time patience in debate to make this journey complete.

Appreciation to my editor John Moriarty for helping in the shaping the work.

Part 3.

Introduction

We all play 'tribal' roles, which evolved over thousands of years and influence our personal, social and cultural values. These are represented in our behaviours in the form of intentions and attitudes. They also reflect our position within our tribal groups. These roles determine the constructive or destructive qualities in our personality and within our society. They were the start of the evolution of modern social and political behaviour.

There are many books about why we behave in the way we do. Few, if any, take you back to the evolutionary tribal, source of our behaviour and how that affects us and society. Most literature on psychology and sociology is focused on the individual; little has produced answers that can give people a working model they can use every day. Much information in this area is provided by professionals who use jargon and medical terminology that often takes power from the individual. This psycho-social model might give people a better understanding of their behaviour and the hope of working toward a positive outcome in lifes challenges. We feel the narrative on behaviour needs to be changed, because what is on offer is not working. As we see in society in general. There is a need for a new perspective that gives more understanding about why we are not achieving a better society from the knowledge we have.

Our approach is to explore our tribal past to gain an understanding of the roles we play today. This book is founded on a simple yet powerful concept, one that can help us to understand our tribal identity relative to ourselves and others. From the moment of our birth, we start to form a tribal identity. It is shaped by the way we are accepted by our family, our peers, and the wider community and by the roles we play and the status we have within these relationships. Our roles and status can often conflict with our sense of self, resulting in dissatisfaction and emotional turmoil. Do the tribes you belong to limit your ability to be yourself?

The book follows a logical and progressive sequence of ideas. First, we explain how our tribal evolutionary behaviours evolved and how they affect our feelings and intentions. Then we show how the tribal roles we play influence the development of our attitudes under different circumstances. We show why the roles people play in relationships can produce harmony or conflict. Exercises help you identify your tribal personality. We also give concise explanations and examples of various personal and interpersonal communications. As you progress through the text you will be able to improve yourself and your relationships in the home, at work and socially. This information will help you to deal with life's many challenges. You will feel more confident about the decisions and actions you take.

Life itself will become more exciting and fulfilling. The information in this book will empower you to see the world from a new perspective that will benefit you and the people around you!

Part One: Discovering the 'characters' within your Tribal Nature

The tribal path to your identity

Have you ever asked yourself the questions, "What roles do I play in life and how do they affect my present and future?" Many of us, at some time or other, have asked ourselves these questions. In the theatre of life, which has many actors, it is often unclear what roles we play and how they represent who we are. Life has become more complex than it was once and relationships have become more dynamic and complicated than they were. If we could recognise and name the roles we play and from this information fashion behaviour appropriate to the situation, we would feel in greater control of our lives. To recognise the roles we play we have to look at humanity's primitive and tribal past, where the roots of our behavioural roles are found. We instinctively know these roles, but they have not been contextualised in a form that enables us to capture their principles.

To distinguish the roles we and others play we need a frame of reference to understand what motivates our behaviour. If we look to our primitive and tribal past, we will see patterns of behaviour that express particular roles that have been consistently present throughout time. In this book we have used the 'characters' of Chief, Warrior, Servant, Mentor and Slave because they indicate specific divisions of behaviour that have been constant in past and present societies. Note the reference to Slave is not used to denigrate but to illustrate the historic ranking of roles that we still see *today*. Each of these 'character' roles has a function in the way we meet our survival needs. We have used 'primitive' to denote basic physical survival behaviours and attitudes in individuals whose agenda are purely self-interested. They developed from the primary instincts, to survive physically by gaining food and water and to build defences to provide shelter. These instincts are found in the Warrior, whose purpose is to acquire and the Chief, who is territorial. These two 'characters are what we have called the primitives because they respond from self-interest – *the survival of the self.* 'Tribal' is used to indicate changes in the Warrior and Chief when those 'characters' act in synergy with the Servant, transforming the attitude of self-interest to one of acting in the interest of self and others within their group. These roles exist in every culture; the functions of each of the roles are similar but are identified by different names. As the roles evolved, so did people's tribal identity, which was necessary for them to act in roles best suited to the interests of the tribe.

The way the 'characters' develop in our personality will depend on our genetic predisposition and our upbringing, and life's many encounters. This will be reflected in the influence or lack thereof of our dealings with others. It is the 'character' roles we play that will influence the type of lives we lead and our status, that is, our perceived importance or lack of importance, in a situation. Sometimes it is hard to get a measure of the relevance of our role in a situation because of the many transactions that take place in an encounter with others. In some circumstances, our roles can be seen clearly; in other situations, they are more or less hidden. Nevertheless, the roles are present in all our interactions with others. It is likely that you can place people you know into these different character roles. It is the stronger 'character' traits that you will be aware of in a person, rather than their other 'characters'. The question is how strongly they express this 'character' and with what frequency. If it is often then that 'character' expresses the way they manage life's issues.

Historically, people have had little choice in the roles they have played. The roles were generally hereditary, with gender and age having an influence on a person's rank. Roles acted to maintain social order and rank. People were required to follow the rules specified by their status and the behaviours acceptable within their society. Unwillingness to accept this requirement carried the risk of punishment, which encouraged people to convey strongly the character roles designated for their class. As roles became more defined, so did the status of the individual. The roles form the structure by which status defines the person's rank within the tribe's hierarchical autocratic approach to social management. It limited an individual's status to a designated class. A Chief was required to organise and control the activities of others; a Warrior to fight and acquire assets to gain prestige; a Servant to serve others to sustain relationships; or a Mentor to give wise counsel; and the Slave was obligated to labour to justify his or her value. When we speak of a 'character' designated to a class it means that 'character' is central to the class it represents, and the other 'characters' are secondary. Democratization has caused a blurring of the roles, where each of us perceives ourself as being equal to others. In reality, this is not true, although the hierarchy of the roles we play is more subtly expressed than it was once. The 'characters' engage in everyday situations, whether in the family, the workplace or the broader society.

Our personality can be defined as a set of 'characters' that possess specific traits affecting our perceptions and motivations in various situations. Often we will express a number of these 'characters' in a transaction, thus indicating our feelings. They will influence the manner in which we communicate and engage with others. The roles we play will indicate our perceived status within the relationship and ultimately the outcome of the situation. Then there are our genes, which can predispose us towards expressing a particular character more strongly than we express the others, forming our temperament, that is, the developmental patterns of behaviour that enables an individual to react to certain situations in a particular way. This developmental process can be observed in early childhood, where children express sociable, assertive or controlling, or shy, passive and sulking behaviours. As these attitudes become more sophisticated, they will indicate the type of character and temperament an individual uses to deal with a situation, as found in the traits of our Warrior (asserting our wants), or Chief (the need to control territory) or Servant (acting to please and appease others to encourage emotional engagement) or as a Slave (accepting the demands of others without question).

If you have ever watched children at Playgroup or school, you will have seen the 'characters' at work in a microcosm of our primitive and tribal behaviour. The primitive behaviour is shown in stealing and bullying, tribal behaviour in co-operative play, seen in caring, sharing and the formation of cliques. There are children who become victims through various styles of negative play. It is understandable that parents become perplexed by some of the behaviours of their children. Their response would probably be, "I don't expect this from my children". We see the individual's self-interest as well as the tribal behaviour being acted out from these early stages. Upbringing can strengthen or weaken either of these aspects of a child's personality. If we understand the primitive and tribal influence on a child's behaviours in the early stages of childhood we can act more effectively in dealing with their inappropriateness. As her or his tribal nature starts to develop in early childhood, the child forms physical bonds and emotional attachments with caregivers and others, helping to develop the Servant 'character' in their personality and giving a developing child the potential to build quality relationships and enabling nurturing that brings safety and in turn builds interdependency. These positive transactions between caregiver and child start the formation of the child's tribal self. As early physical and emotional infantile bonds begin to diminish, it is expected the child will switch to fend for himself or herself. The child's attachment needs will hopefully take a socially adapted form that promotes a positive reaction from others. This is expressed in the pleasing actions of the Servant 'character' in the child, which aim to gain acknowledgement for her or his contribution to others in the group. Early childhood experiences set the foundations for the building blocks on which 'characters'' synergy will form. Synergy occurs when the different traits of the 'characters' are incorporated to advance the socialising and civilising of the primitive nature, as found in the Warrior and Chief.

If we focus on the 'characters' we express and define their influence we can see better how our activities are affected by the roles we play and the worth we place on ourselves. We have all experienced situations in which we have behaved inappropriately. If we know which 'characters' are involved in our communication we can deal with the situation with integrity. Think of the attributes of your 'characters' as an emotional and mental tool kit. You can choose the 'characters' that are best suited to the various situations you find yourself in. If you are required to act as a Chief but express the attributes of a Warrior or Servant, others will know it is not the role they expected you to express. We then become more vulnerable to developing difficulties in the relationship, because others expect us to express a behaviour that is different to that which we have expressed. Most of us will have encountered this situation in some form. A friend may have said to you, "I did not expect you to give up that easily", or, "You surprised me with how well you handled yourself". Most of us monitor other people and are aware of shifts in roles, without knowing the reason for this change in behaviour. Being able to define the 'characters' through the way they communicate and their motives and intentions will give us a better understanding of how our behaviour affects others and vice versa.

Revolution of change in our tribal behaviour

People are no longer limited by expectations that they should exhibit particular roles that were specified to maintain their social class. Changes in society allow a greater flexibility for individuals to choose the roles they play at any social level. But we have developed a new social labelling system – stereotyping – that can be based on genetic disposition, upbringing, personal choices, education, environment and the group we belong to. Stereotyping refers to a collection of personal and group beliefs. Because there is less rigidity in this system people are able to accommodate each other's qualities, allowing a greater synergistic relationship between the 'characters'. The synergy of the 'characters' is important to the growth and maintenance of our tribal identity. A synergy formed between the Warrior and Chief with the Servant transforms our primitive self-interest to a more inclusive relationship forming our tribal nature. The merging of the different traits of each of the 'characters' produces a stronger adaptive capacity that strengthens the survival of the individual and the group. Biologists contend that all social animals, from ants to elephants, have modified their behaviours by restraining immediate selfishness to improve their evolutionary fitness. Character synergy is the way we have modified our self-interest as a survival strategy. It is our Servant in synergy with the Warrior and Chief that restrains our primitive nature.

Each individual has a unique 'character synergistic' personality. That is, they have their own way of expressing their characters. This will show in the strengths and weaknesses of their characters in different environments. If we have a strong Warrior we will be competitive and acquisitive. If the Chief is dominant, then we will have a more controlling and defensive disposition. Whereas in the Servant a sociable and agreeable attitude. The synergistic relationship between the 'characters' gives us our unique personality and our sense of tribalism – the need to be emotionally connected by acting to serve others within our group.

<u>Note:</u> *Synergy between the 'characters' will be dealt with in greater depth in Part Two. It is important to note that the 'characters' represented apply to all genders and ages. Also, at times the previous text will be referenced to help you to keep in mind how the 'characters', both in their singular and synergistic forms, affect your behaviour. This will enable you to clearly identify them within yourself and within transactions with others.*

Introduction to traits and roles of our 'characters'

When you recognise each 'characters'' traits you may feel that you can strongly identify with a particular 'character'. Though we might express one of the 'characters' more frequently than the others, it is unlikely that we will stay in one 'character' all the time because life circumstances will elicit many responses. We are a combination of all the 'characters' in varying degrees. Although one 'character' might be dominant, in specific spheres of our lives the other 'characters' can also manifest themselves. This depends on our sense of security in a given situation. The functions of our 'characters' are to protect, organise, gain resources, form and maintain relationships and give wise counsel.

The traits of the 'characters' are the dynamic forces expressed in varying degrees in our personality. They define the intentions of our communications and actions that can enhance, limit or damage our relationships. When we refer to a Chief, Warrior, Servant or Mentor we are referring to the communication and behaviour expressed by an individual in a certain manner that conveys how they feel in a situation. While we are all made up of a mix of 'characters', it is important to understand the basic characteristics and motivating influences behind each 'character'. By understanding the traits of the 'characters' we can use them as our emotional and mental tool kit to interpret and shape our behaviour in a constructive way.

As you move through the different traits of different 'characters' you will begin to build an impression of how they influence your life. You can explore the context in which you have experience of, or have observed, the 'characters' and the kind of vocabulary and dialogue they would use and specific behaviours they would exhibit, so you can more easily identify their representation in your life. When there is a reference to 'character' personality types it means an individual has a strong predisposition for expressing a specific 'character'. It does not exclude them from expressing other 'characters'.

Primitive Warrior

The primal action of this Character is to conquer physical hunger

If we were strongly influenced by this 'character', we would have no consideration for the feelings or needs of others. Our behaviour might range from conceited to brutish. To get our own way we would not give a second thought to taking advantage of others by exploiting their mental, physical and emotional weaknesses, using deception, manipulation and disguise. If we meet resistance, we may use aggression regardless of the cost to others to acquire what we want. We sometimes mask our intent by feigning empathy to gain an advantage.

This 'character' can cause us to be ruthlessly ambitious, a risk-taker and uncompromising. We see winning as vital, particularly in times of physical conflict. In sporting activities our Primitive Warrior can emerge in the heat of battle. We have all experienced this 'character' in our behaviour or seen it in others. It usually leaves a strong impression of feelings and memories where we feel 'I wish I had handled that differently'. What has been said about this 'character' has not been flattering. Its positive quality can be appreciated in life-and-death situations.

The Primitive Warrior alone can occasionally inadvertently help others, when backed into a corner and forced to fight. This 'character' in combination with the Chief gives the capacity for survival in times of physical threat.

The Primitive Warrior-type personality is uncompromisingly competitive. It is inclined to be short-tempered and to use physical and/or verbal aggression to gain satisfaction by bullying. In disputes Primitive Warriors see others as having the problem. They have a sense of self-entitlement and are extremely unpleasant if they do not get what they want.

The signature of this 'character' is: being totally insensitive, strident and aggressive, ranging from coercive behaviour to brutality. In interpersonal disputes Primitive Warriors will strike the first blow. They are devoid of empathy, deviously opportunistic, unpredictable, spiteful, and manipulative. In conflict situations they are dangerous people to be around.

The Warrior's underlying intention in communication is to show that they are capable of anything to get what is wanted:

"That is not going to stop me!" (*I will challenge any opposition.*)

"I don't care what they say!" (*They are not important.*)

"Don't get in my way!" (*You will pay for it if you do.*)

"Who cares? I'll take it while it's there!" (*I have no obligations to anyone.*)

"I won't do what you say!" (*You have no power over me.*)

"I can do what I like and you can't stop me!" (*I can please myself what I do.*)

"I do it my way!" (*Why should I take notice of you?*)

"If you don't give it to me, I'll take it!" (*I will gain, regardless.*)

"Their loss is my gain!" (*I am the victor.*)

"What's in it for me?" *(I am interested only in my needs).*

An historical illustration of the Warrior's self interest

The Warrior chases off the enemy, assumes the battle is won, then leaves the battlefield in search of the spoils of war. The need to pillage and plunder means out goes good judgement. The Chief discovers too late that the enemy has regrouped: the enemy wins the day. Acts of pillage and plunder have lost many battles.

If the Warrior is ill disciplined or there is no moral leadership, then self-interest often prevails; the focus turns to gaining the spoils of war. When civil disorder takes place in a tribal army, looting can take place. After the Second World War, the Fourth Geneva Convention of 1949 explicitly banned 'pillage' by occupation armies. Individuals who act through their Primitive

Warrior have no sense of the damage they cause to others by their actions.

The Primitive Chief

The principal need for this 'character- is to control and defend his/her own interests

If we were greatly influenced by this 'character' we would have a grandiose sense of self-importance. Our behaviour would range from stubbornness to vindictiveness. We would expect others in our relationship to acquiesce in our demands and support our opinions. Our inherent prejudices (moral, cultural, racial, political) will have a strong influence on the way we defend our opinions and decisions.

There is an underlying anxiety in people who act from this 'character' about their security. To mitigate their feelings they exchange them for dominant behaviour to secure power. If they feel threatened, either physically or emotionally, it causes them to cover up their feelings of inadequacy by using threats or coercion. They enjoy adulation from others. This can amplify their sense of power and invincibility and encourage a greater sense of entitlement.

This is the oldest leadership style, dating back to when the tribes began to take shape. You may have had personal experience of this type of behaviour. It can manifest when a person is acting from a position of power and venting their frustrations, especially when they feel overwhelmed. In such a scenario, they get subordinates to carry out demeaning tasks or demote them as a way of gaining a sense of authority. It is an unproductive behaviour in the long term. Historically the Chief used physical punishment, coercion and conformity in retaining and maintaining ownership and respect for his or her status.

Chiefs see others as being in service to them, not themselves as being in service to others. There are exceptions in acting from the Primitive Chief style of leadership: when conditions are dangerous, applying rigid rules can keep people out of harm's way.

Their deep-seated fear is of being vulnerable to others, whether the threat is real or perceived. They build emotional and physical walls to protect *their* vulnerability. For example, Chiefs often build edifices to proclaim their importance, without considering the cost: *Head Slave reports to the Chief that at the beginning of building the wall, there were 3,000 slaves, and now there are only 1,000 slaves left. "Is the wall complete"? the Chief asks. The Chief is interested only in results, not the emotional and physical cost to others.*

Individuals acting from this 'character' are usually the last to acknowledge that the empire has fallen. They see status, image, and perceived infallibility as strengths; this self-deception produces insensitivity to the physical and emotional issues of others. Many individuals throughout history have used their status for self-interest and this has often brought about their demise. This type of behaviour has been displayed by dictators such as Hitler, Mussolini, and Stalin to maintain their power. They act from their Primitive Chief, expressing prejudice and giving directives in the use of coercion and punishment to maintain conformity to their beliefs.

The Primitive Chief-type personality is uncompromisingly defensive and has a strong need to control others and maintain power. Primitive Chief personalities use the laws of divide and rule by having favourites within their group. They are totally insensitive to the opinions of others. They often make decisions without consultation, expecting others to follow their lead without question. They do not forgive challenges to their authority.

The signature of this 'character' in an individual will express a threatening, harsh tone. Their displeasure can be shown in a number of ways such as a rigid stance, staring eyes, finger pointing or fist clenching and frowning. They are opinionated, defensive, ideological, patronising, authoritative, and demanding. They will use any means to show authority and power, and can make others' lives miserable.

The Primitive Chief's underlying intention in communication is to maintain his or her status regardless of the cost to others:

"I don't care what it costs you, get it done!" (*No price is too high when someone else is paying.*)

"That was an unforgivable act!" (*You will pay for it.*)

"I'm not going to let the issue go!" (*This will be held against you.*)

"There's no excuse for what you have done!" (*You stand condemned.*)

"You've exceeded the boundaries of stupidity!" (*You are totally useless and irresponsible.*)

"Rules are going to be enforced!" (*There are no negotiations.*)

"I'm going to change your attitude if it is the last thing I do!" (*You will do as I say.*)

"Do what I say, not what I do!" (*My status gives me privileges.*)

"I'll see how you perform before giving judgement!" (*I am the final arbiter.*)

"Who do you think you are talking to?" (*Remember your place or you will be sorry.*)

A Note about the primitive 'characters'

The Primitive Warrior and Chief are easy to identify within us all. Any situation where we feel confronted may cause these 'characters' to emerge. A person feeling physically or emotionally threatened will usually react in a manner that reveals predominant primitive traits (as described in the voice, gestures, attitudes and behaviours of the Warrior and Chief previously outlined). The threat may be real or perceived; however, it is our perception that engages the 'characters' we express.

In stressful situations a reaction may result in the Primitive being expressed. For example, many parents are faced with children who pester them and on occasions may respond in an unchecked manner, giving vent to their Primitives. The child may have asked repeatedly to be allowed to do what her or his friends are doing or may have pressured the parent for something she or he wanted while out shopping. Most parents have experienced these scenes. Children challenge the parent's decision to act on their behalf. Finally the parent loses patience and may shout at or even strike the child, unleashing their Primitive Chief to gain control.

Take another situation, in which a salesperson questions your motives for wanting a refund for an item you believe to be faulty. The salesperson suggests that you have not used the product in accordance with the instructions. The suggestion makes you feel unjustly treated, in a confrontational manner and you may lash out with a primitive response. "Are you stupid or what?" "Of course I read the instructions!" The Primitive Chief erupts and anger escalates even more. You may invade the salesperson's space and grab him in a moment of fury. The Primitive Warrior emerges from you unchecked.

In some individuals these primitive 'characters' show sociopathic behaviour; they exhibit narcissism, self-absorption, a sense of importance and exaggerated self-worth. On the cultural front when these characters play a dominant role in the political and social arena of a culture there is a potential for major social up evil.

The Servant

The principal need for this 'character' is to form emotional relationships to gain security

If we were influenced mainly by this 'character', our behaviour would range from seeking approval to pleasing others and working diligently to finish tasks. This action is taken in the expectation that it will encourage others to form emotional attachments that will gain acceptance for us, to fulfil a need for security. The motivation behind this 'character' is to overcome nurturing needs not sufficiently experienced or met in childhood. This can include the fear of rejection, causing us to suspend our own needs and desires so we can meet the wants of others. The emotional attachment of others we crave and the needs and dependence we rely on, form the tribal glue. For any society to work effectively there must be some degree of dependency, conditioning, feeling obligated to others and others being obligated to you to enhance the common good of the group.

Although the Servant connects with others through service, it is the desire to gain acceptance and security that is at the root of the actions. This 'character' defines self by identifying with others and the accepted social norms, in the assumption that those he or she serves will look after his or her interests. This makes such a person vulnerable to exploitation and manipulation. If an individual is constantly seeking to please, he or she becomes vulnerable to the whims of others. Excessive fawning behaviours could engender too much familiarity and even contempt, thus

17

leading to feelings as found in the Slave character – of being unappreciated, of resentment and powerlessness and therefore of feeling excluded from the family or group.

The Servant-type personality has a strong need for acknowledgment of his or her value to the other person's life. The main intent is to gain and maintain support and security through the actions of helping. In turn the Servant strengthens his or her relationships with those who have her or his interests at heart. The Servant avoids engaging in contentious issues and conflicts to maintain the status quo. Servants see the limits of their freedom as a trade-off for security. The signature of this 'character' in an individual will express low and controlled vocal expression with a tendency to whisper. In verbal transactions the Servant prefers others to initiate and will show patience when waiting for a response. Servants are discreet and will demonstrate a desire to be polite and respectful. When given tasks they are compliant, agreeable, reliable and feel duty-bound. They do not initiate, but will make polite suggestions to inform. They can often be trapped within their status level because of the need for acceptance.

The Servant's underlying intention in communication is to gain and sustain a physical and emotional connection:

"I'll do that for you." (*You have more important things to do.*)
"This is what I have been doing, is it all right?" (Are you pleased *with me? Have I done well?*)
"If you don't like what I've done, I'll change it." (*I am flexible towards your needs.*)
"Do you want me to do anything else?" (*I am a willing servant.*)
"I'll put that right for you." (*Nothing is too much trouble.*)

"I see there is more to be done." *(I am mindful of my responsibilities.)*

"I'll wait for your instructions." *(I need to be told what to do.)*

"Would it be helpful if I did that?" *(I am not sure if this is acceptable)*

"What way would you like me to do this...?" *(I need you to give me directions.)*

The Mentor

The Principal need for this 'character' is to find an ethical answer to solving disharmony

If we were strongly influenced by this 'character' we would convey calm and suggest that all points of view be considered before an action is taken. We would reflect on our intentions, feelings, and thoughts and consider the needs of others as well as our own. This 'character' evolves from an ability to be introspective, to view our actions, questioning motives and considering the consequences. This introspection creates the potential for us to rise above the prejudices found in the other 'characters', who are rooted in physical survival. It allows us to remain detached while being helpful. We are able to function with discernment, common sense and goodwill. The Mentor acts as a role model to others, promoting the development of a social conscience.

The Mentor acts in a manner that demonstrates personal conscience, in which consideration is given to actions and their possible effect on others. Then, there is the social conscience, through which this 'character' encourages others to express attitudes that build integrity, cooperation and that promote universal human rights. The Mentor feels close to people, and generally appreciates life. She or he is interested in solving problems; this often includes helping others to find positive outcomes to difficult situations. It is difficult for an individual to express this 'character' in an environment where there are strong emotional tensions and physical hostilities exhibited by the Primitive 'characters'. It is the Mentor who ultimately tries to reach middle ground, no matter how extreme the arguments on either side are. It should be noted here that an individual who responds to conflict is exposed to risk. When our Mentor responds to a conflict situation, we can be vulnerable to blame by one or both sides for lack of resolution, or we may even be accused of further inflaming the conflict. People who put themselves at risk in these circumstances are police officers, ambulance officers, doctors, nurses, social workers, counsellors, community workers and aid workers.

Historically, the Mentor can be seen in people who respond from a higher level of consciousness by encouraging others to reflect and reach their own solutions and by offering alternatives to conflict. Many leaders have exhibited the capacity to act beyond self-interest. Socrates, William Wilberforce, Ghandi, Mother Teresa, Nelson Mandela, Desmond Tutu and many others have expressed these qualities. They believed all human beings have the capacity to reach a higher level of consciousness.

The Mentor-type personality is accepting of themselves and of others as equals. The Mentor's humanistic view of conflicts is that contentious issues can be solved with forgiveness and compromise, by encouraging open-mindedness and reason. Mentors will act without prejudice, using inquiry to explore the motives behind an action. They encourage an ethical approach to resolving the problem. Their objective approach is a counter to the prejudices found in other 'characters', which helps the Mentors see the reality of a situation more clearly than others.

The signature of this Character in an individual will express a well-modulated, questioning and encouraging manner and give information with a calming and reflective tone. Mentors will use a friendly, open, accepting manner that is impartial and ethical. They seek compromise; consider all points of view beyond personal and tribal interests; remain objective in conflicts and keep confidences. The Mentor is an excellent communicator and mediator, is encouraging, considerate and patient and focuses on reducing distress and can acknowledge her or his own humanity, vulnerability and strengths. The Mentor is extremely significant in many ways, adding compassion, empathy and charity in many situations.

In a tribal context, consider a nomadic tribe struggling to survive. The essential basic needs are to gain shelter, water and food for the tribe and this requires the co-operation of all tribal members. For a tribe to survive in the long term, the Mentor's level of reasoning needs to emerge and to consider survival as a species and the consequences of tribal activity within the group and their impact on the environment for their long-term well-being and survival.

The Mentor's stimulate the social conscience:

"If you do this, what will be the effect on others." *(Have you thought about the consequences?)*
"Is this a wise thing to do?" *(Have you enough knowledge to make this decision?)*
"Is it a fair way of doing things?" *(Is honesty being shown in this issue?)*
"Do you consider it best to leave the situation to sort it out?"*(Is it appropriate to step in?)*

"Does the action go against what you feel?" (*Are you being honest with yourself and others?*)

"There is the option to do the right thing." (*You have a choice in what you do.*)

"With every action there is a responsibility." (*Are you prepared to accept the consequences?*)

"Change can be beneficial and also painful." *(There is a choice between growth and comfort.)*

"Has the proposal been carefully checked out to see that everyone benefits?" *(Do you need to consult others?)*

The principal 'characters' – Chief, Warrior and Servant – ensure the physical survival of the individual within the tribe by providing shelter, food and co-operation. The Mentor provides a contrast that enables us to see the intent behind our own actions and those of others. By giving wise counsel, the Mentor promotes and encourages respectful and responsible behaviour.

This diagram illustrates the reaction to a leader who demands tone, can be dissent.

The Characters will reveal themselves through:

> Type of words used.
> Tone Voice, volume, intensity, inflection
> Body posture, gestures and facial expression
> Which may give and indication

The following shows how our 'characters' empower us and gaining and ensuring security. What empowers our 'characters':

- Mentor- bringing harmony
- Chief – power and responsibility
- Warrior –self-determination
- Servant – acceptance, approval and regard for service

The diagram is a division of attitudes of the primary Characters

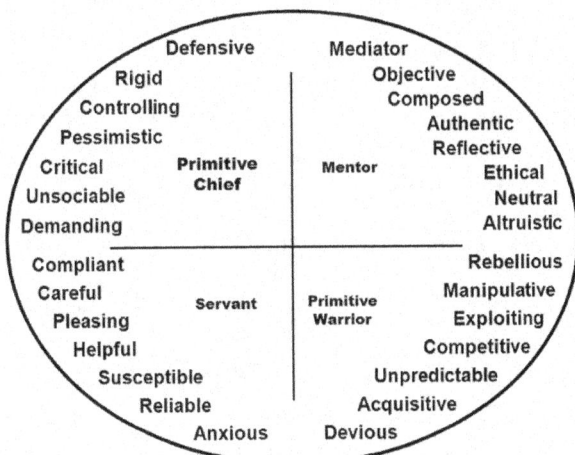

Figure 1: Traits of the 'characters'

What the 'character's' function is:

- Chief – to maintain power over territory by cohesion and force if necessary
- Warrior – to achieve power, rewards and independence through assertion and aggression
- Servant – to seek emotional attachment through service
- Mentor – to create balance through reflection and ethical behaviour

Diagram of traits of the 'characters'

The Diagram shows the four primary Character traits that provide us with behaviours to attain our biological, physical, and emotional needs to survive.

The principal 'characters' are the:

- Primitive Warrior who adapts, acquires and creates opportunities
- Primitive Chief who controls and organises
- Servant who serves others to gain emotional attachment and security
- Mentor who brings reflective counsel and ethics to situations
- The Slaves in our
- personality *(Infantile Slave* and *Recalcitrant Slave)*

The Infantile Slave

This is not a 'character' in the true sense; it is a sub-state of the Servant, with no status in a relationship other than dependency.

If we are greatly influenced by this state, we would avoid social interplay with others, other than to serve a menial role. It arises from early childhood dependency issues and possible abuse. In this state, we would be submissive, doing others' bidding even when requests are unreasonable. If abused we will excuse the abusive behaviour to avoid isolation and abandonment. It is a state of extreme dependency. We would be dependent on others to manage our lives. We may feel trapped by our circumstances and the fear of emotional disconnection, which means having to relinquish any personal autonomy.

This sense of powerlessness, real or perceived, can cause mild to extreme anxiety and depression. When facing this extreme sense of enslavement, it is difficult for someone to access their other 'characters'. An outside agent may be required to awaken the reality of their situation to guide them towards the discovery and realisation of their other 'characters' that can be utilised in a reasoned way. There are situations where people who experience this state can snap, expressing an uncensored Primitive Warrior showing rage, resulting from hurts and abuse, suppressed over a period of time. After the release of these feelings, there can be a cathartic experience and also feelings of grief and guilt. It is the grief and guilt that sabotage a feeling of freedom, causing them to go back to the same state of powerlessness.

The Infantile Slave-type personality sees his or her life as having little importance. They will suffer in silence and fear negative reactions and are emotionally over-sensitive to their surroundings. Infantile Slaves easily give way to the whims and wants of others. They have difficulty in making everyday decisions without an excessive amount of reassurance from others. They have difficulty in expressing disagreement as the fear of losing support or approval is too great. The signature in this Character can express a weak and pleading tone that can be perceived as whining. Infantile Slaves show little animation and avoid any attention. In disputes they try to avoid involvement. If they become involved they will resign themselves to being at fault. They are obedient, amenable, timid and easily brought to tears.

The Infantile Slaves' intention within communications is to gain sympathy for their plight and to reduce gaining attention that may bring them into conflict:

"I am fearful of them coming home." *(I feel panicky.)*
"Faith will take me from this." *(Hope is all I have.)*

"I try not to upset them." *(I fear the consequences.)*

"I don't think I can cope." *(I feel powerless.)*

"They never give me any peace." *(There's no time for me.)*

"If there is any sickness going around, I'll get it." *(I always have to be very careful.)*

"I cry at the least little thing." *(I need attention.)*

"I know they've got faults and this causes me to grieve but I love them." *(I am dependent on them.)*

"If anything is going to happen, it will happen to me and it won't be good." *(I can prove life is against me.)*

The Recalcitrant Slave

This state is not a 'character' in the true sense: it is a sub-state of the Primitive Warrior, where the anger is channelled by secretive and subversive behaviour.

If we were to act from this state, we would be experiencing feelings of resentment towards those whom we think have control over our lives or those by whom we feel threatened. We would be unable to express ourselves openly; this often causes frustration expressed in revengeful behaviour acted out surreptitiously. This can take the form of giving the impression we accept a situation while engaging in subterfuge such as resisting following instructions, deflecting blame, or finding immediate excuses for not fulfilling obligations, and in the use of sabotage. There is also a tendency to engage in innuendo and gossip, with the intention of defaming someone. Situations in which this state can emerge include when we experience changes in our circumstances or when we feel disenfranchised. We may feel discriminated against or feel a loss of status or a breakdown in relationships. There are other situations that breed discontent, such as constantly being asked to justify decisions taken, or when a person in a power position changes the conditions of the relationship without consultation. When we can no longer hold back our feelings of resentment they will find expression in the Primitive Warrior, exploding into open conflict. If we are unable to find a healthy avenue to discharge the built-up resentment, the stress produced may lead to mental, emotional and physical illness.

The Recalcitrant Slave's feelings often stem from early childhood, in which a child is exposed to conflicting messages of obligations required by a parent figure and her or his own needs for independence. That parent-child conflict can carry over into adulthood as resentment, manifest in divisive behaviour such as manipulation or secretiveness to counter the demands of others. This can find its expression in failed relationships. Where there are unresolved issues, individuals may use divide and rule tactics to gain the upper hand in recompense for their suffering. Family breakups can be areas where this state may manifest itself.

People in positions of power can exhibit this state. Often they fear a loss of position or feel alienated in their status. Their inability to be open in a relationship comes from fear of appearing weak. They will employ divisive approaches in using their power, such as deception and manipulation of others to promote their own agenda or gain revenge. They will manipulate to bring down anyone whom they consider a threat.

The case of the whistle-blower acting from this state to gain justice through revenge can benefit others indirectly. When opportunities arise to gain revenge for feelings of dissatisfaction within their organisation, they do this by highlighting criminal or socially irresponsible behaviour. This type of behaviour has also brought down empires, benefiting no one. There is, however, the whistle-blower who acts from her or his Mentor 'character', seeing that action needs to be taken to right a wrong without prejudice and to reduce harm. If the behaviour comes from the Mentor, the intent is different – Mentors see the damage that may be caused or is being caused to others as the important factor for acting on the information they have.

The Recalcitrant Slave-type personality is often resentful and maliciously calculating. Recalcitrant Slaves feel others have treated them unfairly or are conspiring against them. They will exhibit behaviours that hide their real feelings and intent, which can drive them to petty or major sabotage. They may even plan, waiting to take revenge to gain satisfaction for pain they have experienced, either real or perceived. The vagaries of dealing with this 'character' can leave others confused and vulnerable.

The signature of this 'character' can show all the behaviours expected of a reasoned person. It is what Recalcitrant Slaves don't say in the conversation that hides the feelings they have towards a person. Their dialogue can be ambiguous and withhold information that may assist the person they feel resentful towards. After conflict they may brood or be short-tempered, depending on the outcome. They may vent their anger through gossip and may employ innuendo to draw attention to the weaknesses, vices and follies of others. They can express a defiant tone when upset, be flippant, furtive and reticent.

The Recalcitrant Slaves' underlying intention in communication is to settle old scores:

"I haven't taken all this for nothing." *(I need to gain something.)*
"They have put me down for too long." *(I need justice.)*
"They don't know I know." *(I will reveal their secrets.)*
"They have not heard the last of this." *(I will surprise them.)*
"They will regret what they have done." *(They will have to answer for it.)*
"I can wait, time is on my side." *(Patience has its own rewards.)*
"I gave good service and all I got was abuse." *(I am aware of the injustice so watch out.)*
"They don't know who they are dealing with." *(I can be ruthless.)*
"I will get my own back one day and they will wonder what happened." *(Revenge will be sweet.)*

Scenarios: Festering emotions

In the following scenarios we show different situations in which the 'characters' we have described are often expressed. Someone you know has experienced similar situations. Try to identify the characters before you read the conclusions in italics at the end of the scenarios.

Scenario 1: Being overlooked

Jordan is the middle child in a family of three. His older brother can do no wrong and his younger sister is treated as special. He feels jealous and resentful of his siblings, and he also feels a sense of injustice because he is sure he is punished more than they are. He feels left out and keeps his head down to avoid trouble as much as he can, and withdraws socially.

As a young adult, Jordan meets Megan and marries her. Their marriage is good until the arrival of their first son. Megan is engaged in taking care of the baby and Jordan begins to feel shut out. Jordan becomes demanding, abrupt and short-tempered with Megan. Megan feels victimised by his constant mood changes and she often breaks down in tears.

Jordan had repressed his childhood vulnerability and jealous resentments (Recalcitrant Slave). His childhood experiences have influenced how he responds to Megan and the new baby. Jordan feels the same now as he felt as a child, a sense of exclusion which gives him tremendous emotional discomfort. He vents in angry outbursts (Primitive Chief). Megan (Infantile Slave) is powerless, captive to her unpredictable circumstances.

Scenario 2: Used and abused

Clive worked for Smith & Co as a supervisor for twelve years. When his departmental head suddenly left, Clive is asked to temporarily fill the position. He successfully runs the department for two months because of his practical administrative skills. He decides to apply for the permanent position but is informed that they require someone with higher academic qualifications. His boss tells him he prefers him to remain in his previous position, as he was doing such a good job.

The newly hired head of department, Mike, exhibits an 'I know it all,' attitude. Clive decides not to offer him any support. Mike experiences great difficulty with his new job because, despite his academic qualifications, his practical abilities do not measure up to the requirements of the position.

Clive expects that his broad knowledge of the department and successful management there of would give him an added advantage and place him ahead of the other applicants. Mike's superior attitude (Primitive Chief), coupled with Clive's disappointment at being passed over, brings out Clive's Recalcitrant Slave.

From Servant to Slave

The Servant role can sometimes be confused with that of the Slave as they both provide service. The difference between them is that the Servant feels committed to serve others and the Slave feels obligated. The Servant feels appreciated and acknowledged for her or his contribution, which affirms a sense of tribal identity. This validation produces a sense of belonging and a further willingness to serve. If however, an individual feels her or his service is not recognised by others, he or she will feel unappreciated and alienated. Feelings can be real or perceived; either way, alienated feelings can engender a number of responses, from the Infantile Slave submitting to the situation and turning inwards, damaging a person's mental health, to venting resentments through the Recalcitrant Slave, who will find expression in deception. If the Primitive Warrior emerges resentment will be vented through aggression.

We can become a Slave without being aware of it. This can occur by degrees, slowly and subtly. This behaviour can have its roots in childhood. The Servant and Slave are by their very definition *powerless*. Both are subjected to the will and wishes of others. There is also the fear of rejection. The Servant experiences recognition and acceptance where the Slave feels rejected. If the Servant or Slave is dominant in a person's life they can be prone to expressing the Primitives (Warrior and Chief). When they experience a prolonged period of stress, falling back to their primitive responses is the way they get out of the feeling of being trapped.

This fear of rejection is very much connected to dependency needs. Fears and neediness can cause an individual to agree to a situation that they are not completely happy about. For example, two people have a mutual agreement on sharing transportation to take the children to a particular activity. After a short time, one of the parents starts to renege on fully fulfilling their part of the agreement. If this continued for a long period of time, then you have a culturally established arrangement, where one of the parties continues to not fulfil the agreement and the other allows it to continue. On the physical level they accept the situation, on the emotional level they feel used. They cannot challenge the other person's position for fear of them being upset. This perspective is to hide their fear of rejection. When forming a relationship, it is important in the early stages to establish boundaries and ways of dealing with conflicts that arise when these have been infringed. If one of the partners in the relationship accepts the behaviour of the other partner on the physical level, but on the emotional level feels aggrieved and allows the situation to continue, this often produces fertile ground for conflict. If the other party is not aware of the issues in their relationship and accepts everything as normal, it becomes part of the culture of the relationship. It is difficult to break cultural habits. The person who is feeling aggrieved and powerless will either continue to accept the situation (Slave) or, if resentment builds, at some point they will express their Primitive Warrior, which will bring about a state of uproar, often leading to a blaming game. At this point the relationship may fall apart. It is important when forming a relationship to establish a reference point that individuals can use to make corrections to the way the relationship is developing.

In these types of dynamics when the person expresses their Primitive Warrior the relationship has reached a point where it is hard to change unless each individual is able to see things from the other's perspective, which relies on the use of Mentor qualities: the ability to step back and review what harm is being caused, what has occurred and how it can be mutually changed so both individuals can feel comfortable and see the gains in maintaining the relationship.

Scenario 1: A child's response to a demand

> I'm out with my friends and you tell me to come home. It's not fair! I never get to do what I want! Why did I have to come home and clean my room? I like the way it is".

When a child considers a parent has unreasonable expectations the child's feelings of anxiety can intensify. In this scenario, the child feels like a 'slave', powerless and put-upon. It is important to address parental expectations of the child's behaviour. Parents should explain to the child that there are requirements of children too and they need to follow rules, as this keeps them safe and teaches them civility. If a child feels repeatedly treated as a Slave, without any recourse or permission to respond, he or she may develop a victim complex or become rebellious.

> Following the unexpected breakdown of her relationship, Marlene stops going to work and spends most of her time in bed. Unable to cope with daily life, she depends on Simon, her ten-

year-old son, to look after his younger brother and sister. Simon does his best to help his mother by bringing her cups of tea and going to the shops for food, but he is met with disapproval and even violence if his errands take too long. Simon misses going to school and playing with his friends and as the days wear on, he yells more frequently and furiously at his younger siblings.

Marlene feels powerless as an Infantile Slave and is unable to cope with her circumstances. She compensates for her feelings of powerlessness by asserting her Primitive Chief by controlling and punishing Simon. Simon's needs for approval drives him to try hard to please her and carry out her demands, while feeling hurt by her behaviour as an Infantile Slave. Forced into a position of having power over his younger siblings, he exhibits his Primitive Chief and Primitive Warrior, also to compensate for his sense of powerlessness as a Slave. This can become a conditioned response in time of stress.

Knowing our vulnerability

Some of us have found ourselves in the role of the Slave and experienced injustice and unkindness, whether intended or not. We can learn how to stop the process that makes us feel like a Slave. This begins with observing the roles we and others play in our transactions. Once we are able to do this, we can control our behaviour and feel more empowered. A sense of power comes from knowing ourselves, even if only temporarily and in specific situations. This enables us to build on our successes.

Identifying the 'characters' in our communication

There are various ways you can observe a Character's communication within oneself and in others. This is achieved by observing facial expressions, gestures, words we use, tone of voice and general attitude. What you observe and the way you interpret the responses from others will depend on the strengths and vulnerabilities you feel. By learning to identify your Character's responses you can improve your communication skills and relationships. You may be able to understand others' assumptions, attitudes, and prejudices. If you learn how to observe the Characters, you will be able to deal appropriately with any given situation.

Below there are questions that can help clarify how much we feel a member of our tribes.

- [ ] When out socially do you feel ill at ease and vulnerable?
- [ ] Do your problems become the main focus of a conversation?
- [ ] Are you drawn to discussing negative issues?
- [ ] Do you hold onto hurt feelings?
- [ ] Do you feel you're upbringing is to blame for your problems in life?
- [ ] Do you gossip?
- [ ] Do you find satisfaction when you hear negative information about people you do not like.
- [ ] Do you talk about your own problems in most conversations with others?
- [ ] Does blaming others make you feel better?
- [ ] Do you have a tendency to make others take responsibility for you?
- [ ] When hurt by others do you wait for opportunities to get even?
- [ ] Do you feel you always seem to end up with the short straw?
- [ ] Do you feel others do not really understand you?
- [ ] Do you sacrifice your needs so others get what they want?

☐ Do you believe others in your relationship have an easier life than you?

☐ If problems arise, do you avoid having to make a decision?

☐ Do you avoid telling people how you feel, particularly when they have upset you?

☐ Do you feel the need to make people aware of what a difficult life you have had or are having?

Mark the boxes you feel reflect your perceptions of the Characters that are dominant in your personality.

☐ a. Warrior – ambitious, striving to acquire, achieve autonomy and get ahead

☐ b. Chief – organising and controlling

☐ c. Servant – serving, supporting and seeking to be accepted by others

☐ d. Mentor – a counsellor to people who find themselves in difficulties

☐ e. Slave – feeling exploited and dumped on

Write down your answers to the following questions and then explore your feelings about the answers you gave:

Have you ever been a Servant and ended up a Slave?

_____

_____

If you became a Slave, how did you feel and respond?

_____

_____

What situation brings out your Primitives?

_____

_____

Which 'characters' did you mainly display in your childhood?

_____

_____

In your present relationships, which 'characters' are dominant?

_____

_____

Are the 'characters' you usually express mostly appropriate to the situation? If not which one is inappropriate?

_____

_____

In a conflict situation do you walk away, apologise even when you are not at fault or fight back

_____

_____

Past events that interplay with present transactions

Past traumatic events can contribute to tension and emotional issues occurring in the present. They can distort our perception of the reality of the situation. Stored-up 'past' feelings can be vented in present situations. This can engender an expression of the Primitives, damaging relationships that have nothing to do with previous events. If an individual's Servant is in play they will resign themselves to the outcome, whereas a well-developed Mentor will approach the situation using reasoning. The scenario below illustrates how a past event influences the Characters we play and their point of view on the events. See if you can identify the Character roles each individual is playing.

Scenario: Effect of past events

Scenario 1: Chain reaction

Jason is busy working when he is approached by his manager and angrily reprimanded for a mistake that he has not made. Before Jason has a chance to explain, his boss's telephone rings. The boss waves him away. It is after 5 o'clock and, fed up, Jason goes home.

Ann, Jason's partner, has had an equally frustrating day at work and is now home with their teething toddler. It is dinner time, and there's no time for her to put her feet up as she has to get on with the dinner.

Jason arrives home and before Ann can get out a word of welcome, he asks, "Is dinner ready?" He states that he's had a hard day. Jason's comments add to Ann's feelings of frustration of being overloaded.

Jason gets a beer from the fridge, sits down in front of the television, and asks "When is dinner, I'm hungry!" Ann apologises for not having dinner ready.

Their other child, Sam, runs into the kitchen covered in mud. Ann loses her temper and yells at Sam, telling him he's a bloody nuisance, and to get outside and get cleaned up before coming back in. Sam goes out, slamming the door, shouting, 'I'd rather live at Joe's house than here!'

In this scenario, we see the chain reaction of 'character' roles: Jason feels wounded like a Slave by his boss, who expresses his Primitive Chief. Ann also feels dismissed and hurt like a Slave. Sam feels condemned by his mother. He rebels, expressing his Primitive Warrior. This scenario shows how each person can become the victim of one event.

The way in which we communicate – the intent, word choices, tone of voice and body stance can indicate the Characters involved. What we say may indicate that prior events or discussions are hiding the true reason behind our behaviour. We may have been in situations where we felt we were unfairly treated, causing us to assert ourselves and defend our current position because these past hurts have not been resolved. There can be underlying issues that the Characters express in the present situation.

Scenario 1: Hidden agendas

Lynn and Jeff have been going out together for six months. Whenever Susan, a close friend of Lynn, meets with them, Jeff makes fun of her in a sarcastic way. Susan feels hurt and annoyed by Jeff's remarks. When she speaks to Lynn about Jeff's behaviour, Lynn laughs it off saying it is just his way of being friendly.

Jeff sees Susan as a threat to his control over Lynn (Primitive Chief). He successfully uses social banter (Primitive Warrior) to alienate and disarm her to ensure he remains the dominant influence in Lynn's life. Susan complains to Lynn about Jeff's behaviour. Lynn shows lack of understanding. This arouses feelings of insecurity and resentment in Susan (Slave).

The scenario demonstrates the subtleties behind the intent, words and actions of the 'characters' playing in this situation. They leave potential for misunderstanding and conflict. That is why it is important to review the experience and the 'characters' involved, thereby gaining a better understanding of what has occurred.

Dialogue that expresses the 'characters'

The language that we express in transactions can produce varied responses from different 'characters'. The following examples show different dialogues between people. These examples are by no means exhaustive because we engage in so many different kinds of transactions every day, but they demonstrate interactions we are all familiar with.

If a person who has responsibility for others expresses his or her Primitive Chief, he or she will make a request in a demanding tone. This can elicit several responses. The person being addressed might respond through her or his Primitive Chief in a defensive way: "I don't like your attitude. It's your problem, take responsibility for it." Or the person might act defiantly from her or his Primitive Warrior: "Don't speak to me like that! Go to hell!" If the Servant responds, the person will comply without feeling hurt; whereas the Slave will comply but feel hurt or resentful.

The Mentor queries the reasoning behind the need for urgency, while showing concern for the person expressing a Primitive 'character', acknowledging the strong feelings but trying to elicit more information as to why this approach has been used. The Mentor tries to put the situation into context to achieve a fair and realistic outcome; and allows all parties to be reflective about their position so a common goal can be gained. When discussion is initiated by an individual expressing his or her Primitive Chief, there is potential for conflict. This will often engender strong feelings of resentment. Then there are those who will agree to the demands *while at the table,* then complain about their treatment afterwards (a Slave response).

Internal dialogues

It is not what others say that causes us grief: it is our interpretation. From our interpretation we may act from our 'characters' either instinctively or thoughtfully. If we act instinctively, we limit our choices, with the potential that we might express our Primitives. A considered response gives us a greater understanding of the situation. Our 'characters' constantly interpret and evaluate our daily experiences. The degree to which we understand our own expectations and the expectations of others will determine how our 'characters' react. Also, our own sense of security or insecurity affects every situation we find ourselves in.

There exists a constant internal dialogue between our 'characters'. We may or may not be aware of this, even though the dialogue has a powerful effect on our lives. When our internal 'characters' are in conflict, inappropriate behaviours may occur. That is, if we have unresolved issues from the past our present responses could be inappropriate or out of proportion to the current situation. Examples of the types of internal conversations an individual may have with themselves within their characters' dialogue when responding to feelings of failure include the Chief admonishing oneself, "That was a stupid thing for me to do!"; the Servant, concerned about the consequences, saying, "I couldn't help it, what should I do to put it right?"; the Warrior, taking no responsibility for the issue, declaring, "I don't care, it's not my problem!" and the Mentor, accepting that we are human, "Everybody makes mistakes, how can we avoid repeating them?"

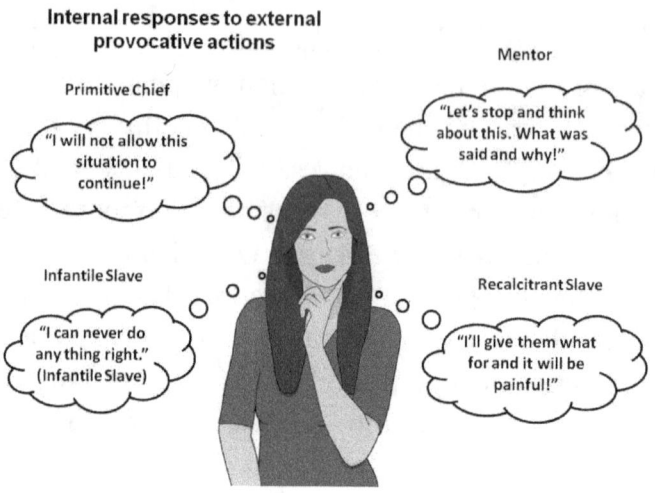

In an external verbal attack by someone saying; "You're stupid! You can't even do the simplest of jobs!", an individual may respond from their Mentor, if developed sufficiently, can help us deal with internal conflicts and possible emotional self-harm by bringing balance to the internal conversation. This is achieved by questioning and reasoning. If they respond from his or her Primitive Chief by saying, "Maybe you need to give better instructions!" or from his or her Primitive Warrior, "Will verbally responde by you're the stupid one!"; or from the Infantile Slave with a self-condemning response; "I know I was stupid". The Recalcitrant Slave may blame others or want revenge, whereas the Mentor would ask the reason for the statement so as to give a measured response.

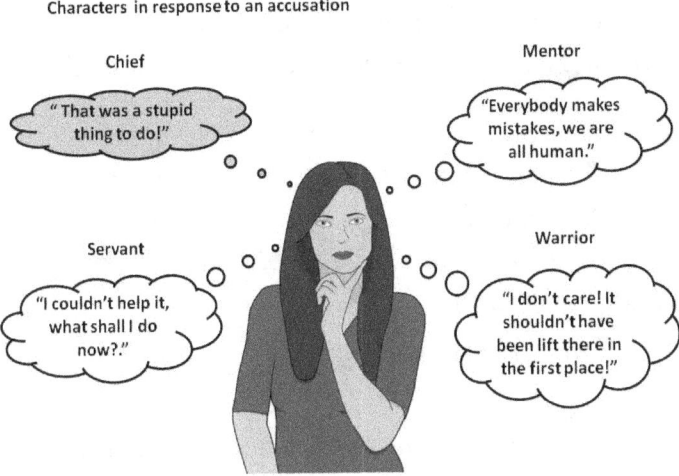

Internal Dialogue of the Primitive
Characters in response to an accusation

Chief
"That was a stupid thing to do!"

Mentor
"Everybody makes mistakes, we are all human."

Servant
"I couldn't help it, what shall I do now?."

Warrior
"I don't care! It shouldn't have been lift there in the first place!"

The positive use of internal conversations is a way of exploring different approaches to problems, utilising the 'characters' and trying various internal dialogues to find an appropriate solution that best fits the situation. Ask the reasons why something happened by examining feelings and thoughts. "What could I have done positively to make a difference?" This question comes from the Mentor. By exploring your feelings and thoughts you can relieve tension, giving yourself time to reflect and build a positive internal dialogue that affirms yourself. The approach, "I am always open to improvement, I try to act with good intentions" will reduce self-abusive dialogue such as, "I'm a fool, I'm always making mistakes!" Both of these statements come from your Slave state. Internal dialogue such as, "You stupid idiot!" or "You'll never learn!" come from your Primitive Chief. This can cause further internal tension that may leave you open to expressing your Primitive 'characters' or your Slave state.

Examples of Internal Dialogue

(1) Johnny buys a car which turns out to be a lemon. His internal response could be any or all of the following:

You're always making stupid decisions! (Admonishing Chief)

That salesman is really going to be sorry! (Revengeful Warrior)

I'm always making stupid decisions! (Slave)

Don't be so hard on yourself. You can learn from this experience. (Mentor)

(2) Jane reluctantly agrees to be a member of a business committee. After agreeing, she feels powerless and her delayed internal response is: *Oh why on earth did I agree to do that when I didn't want to?* (Slave)

(3) Chris is told by his boss 'Get your act together or you're down the road!' Chris responds by walking out. His internal response is: *He can't tell me what to do – stuff him!* (Warrior)

Our thoughts and feelings about unresolved issues can create physical, mental and emotional tensions. Any one of our 'characters' may dominate our internal dialogue, making it difficult to get a true understanding of issues. If our Mentor is engaged we will have the opportunity to partially or wholly release the tension. This can be achieved by re-visiting the circumstances and responding with appropriate internal dialogue:

"It is human to make mistakes", or *"That didn't work out. What options do I have now?"* or *"What can I learn from this so that I can respond differently in a similar situation?"*

When we listen to our internal dialogue or verbalise it, we become aware of our conditioned, automatic responses and are more able to consider our humanness, responsibility and the appropriateness of our actions and to question what is our goal, intent and desired outcome. This can give us the opportunity to change any reactive responses we used in the past to one appropriate to the present.

Part Two: Tribalisation of the Primitive 'characters'

Part 1 describes how our sense of self and even our own survival can be understood by examining our internal 'characters', the primary nature of the Primitive in our survival and the role of the the Servant and Mentor in forming society. We also discussed the Slave state and how it inhibits our sense of self.

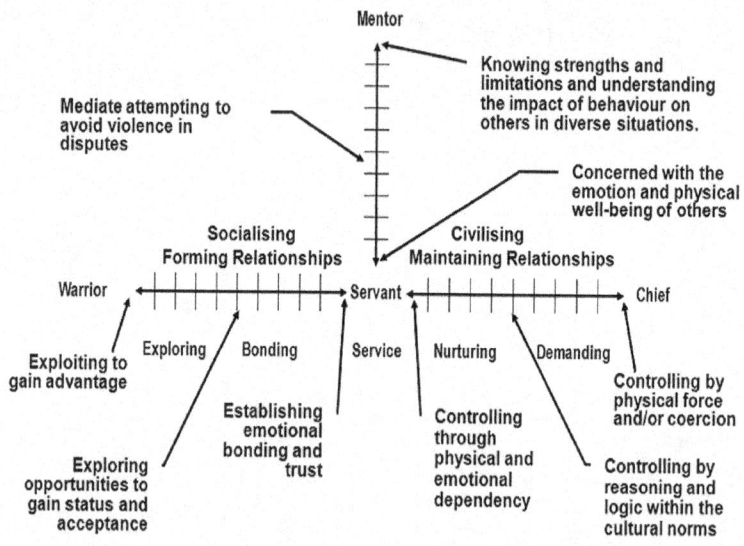

In this part of the work we explore the synergy between the 'characters', the complexities they introduce to our personalities and how that synergy blends the basic traits of the various ''characters' in subtle ways, which gives us our unique personality. First, the Primitive nature of humans was affected by our evolution into more communal (tribal) beings. Of necessity, we have learned to co-operate with others as we have developed a more civilised and socialised approach to relationships. Our

Servant is the catalyst in this transition from a self-oriented being to a tribal one.

The Primitive self is derived from our early evolutionary reactions to a hostile environment that called for behaviours that maximised the ability to survive. This required a black and white response to situations of life and death. When individuals started to form tribal groups, forming allegiances and alliances and serving each other's interest, social reasoning started to develop. A more sophisticated approach to behaviour, building of trust, negotiation and accommodation was required. This transformation produced complex psychological processes that created an internal synergy between 'characters', incorporating the self's needs with the needs of others. This synergy is strengthened by social conditioning that starts in early childhood. The child learns what their parents feel is good and what they feel is bad – "what is to be desired and avoided". The interchange between parent and child elicits certain 'character' responses that build synergy between the 'characters' within the child. This synergistic development is brought about by teaching children to respond in a manner generally approved of by the society to which they belong.

Negative attitudes are more likely to reduce 'character' synergy in an individual, whereas positive social conditioning can produce strong emotional bonds and patterns of behaviour that encourage 'character' synergy and Mentor qualities. These modify the inherent primitive impulses through social reasoning, interpreting and constructing behaviours to accommodate both self-interest and the interests of others and help us navigate the complexities of a situation.

There is also an inherent 'character' predisposition within an individual that can cause unstructured and impulsive behaviour.

This indicates that the synergy between the internal 'characters' is fragile, particularly under stress or in mental illness, which can cause a person to exhibit their Primitive 'characters' through inconsiderate and aggressive behaviours. They may express their Infantile Slave, finding it difficult to do things for themselves. Both the Primitive and Slave responses override the socialising qualities found in 'character' synergy and in Mentor behaviour that allow us to act in a responsible way.

Our inherent nature and social conditioning influence the way the 'characters' are expressed in our personalities. The 'character' that is dominant in the synergistic relationship will be shown in the text as, for example, Warrior/Servant. The '/' symbol shows this is a synergistic relationship, and the dominant 'character' is placed first.

The traits and roles of 'characters' in synergy

The diagram below shows the synergistic relationships between 'characters' and how they contribute to the four stages of a relationship; 1) engagement, 2) building trust and intimacy, 3) building a social framework, 4) preparing the next generation to build its relationships. These states can easily apply to expanding an enterprise.

To put in diagram In Warrior/Servant synergy the Warrior adds excitement to the Servant's need for emotional connection. Their combined traits establish the initial interest in exploring the potential for a relationship.

In Servant/Warrior synergy the Servant adds the need to build empathy and intimacy, which is enlivened by the Warrior's need for pleasure. This combination of traits engenders thoughts and feelings that build emotional closeness and trust.

48

The linking of these 'characters' creates complementary and contradictory aspects of our personality. The Servant forms the emotional glue and the Warrior provides mental agility and assertiveness. In this relationship the Servant moderates the opportunistic behaviour of the Warrior 'character' and keeps us within civil and social boundaries. In Chief/Servant synergy the Chief adds conviction and a sense of power to the Servant's need for reassurance. In this combination of traits the Chief and Servant form a relationship that builds teamwork and strengthens group identity.

In Servant/Chief synergy the Servant adds nurturing to the Chief's practical need to maintain security. In those who display this synergy strongly, the synergy is often formed from their early childhood development. People who are strongly influenced by this synergy are emotionally dependent on tribal values and cultural norms to give them a sense of security. They see the tribal values as important in preparing the next generation for their roles and in building a sense of obligation to the tribe.

The Warrior/Servant

Tests for the benefits of a relationship

In Warrior/Servant synergy we will assert our interest in engaging in a relationship. We use our mental and physical prowess with the desire to impress and charm. The intention of this behaviour is to show that we are a suitable person for others to form a relationship with. In childhood this is seen when a child tries to impress a sibling, peer or parent – "Look what I have done" and garners praise to affirm her or his sense of identity

In this synergy the Warrior is still acquisitive, but the focus is no longer on satisfying self-needs. This Warrior drive is transformed by the Servant in the synergy, forming the desire to pursue activities that show the person to be competent. This competence serves to attract the interest of others in a socially engaging way. The Warrior/Servant tends to be outgoing, competitive, self-promoting, high spirited, and driven by material needs and the need for status. The Warrior/Servant is a great asset in situations where there is a need for team solidarity and camaraderie, and particularly where there is a need for competitive courage. Warrior/Servants can have a deep need to be in charge, seeking to acquire status and prestige to gain followers, ultimately to become a Chief.

If an individual expresses the negative qualities of the Warrior/Servant, he or she tends to challenge social norms to draw attention to the ways in which they are different. In striving to gain social status they will project a material image: property, boats, cars, clothes, etc. They generally have narcissistic qualities. They are highly competitive, to compensate for their lack of self-esteem and their anxiety and intimacy problems. Often they will avoid involving themselves in external emotional issues, as this may connect them with their own personal fears. If rebuffed by an individual or a group, they deny their true feelings by shrugging it off (*It's their loss, not mine!*).

Warrior/Servant type personalities can be self-promoting and enterprising; they seek to gain personal and professional status. They initiate relationships by exploring physical and mental strengths and exploiting weaknesses in a potential relationship. They are ambitious go-getters enjoying the action of the pursuit. They may persuade or seduce us to get their way and can be extravagant in order to make an impression. In any competitive activity they will strive to excel as a way to make their mark. They do not like to be concerned with details, only with the bigger picture. They may go to extreme lengths to impress others in building their persona.

The signature of these 'characters' in synergy in an individual is a boisterous tone, a tendency to be very talkative, and being expressive. They are enthusiastic, animated, use the whole body and make strong gestures with their hands to express themselves. Their risk-taking is aimed at social acceptance and involves being engaging, boastful, sarcastically humorous, and flirtatious.

Some occupations of people with this 'character' synergy are war journalist, artist-actor, stunt person, marketing, sales person, sports player, mortgage and investment broker, interior/exterior designer, public relations person, advertising, entertainer, fashion designer, court lawyer, body builder.

The Warrior/Servant's underlying intention in communication is to take the initiative with bravado and optimism

"I've got a new idea." *(I am prepared to try new things.)*

"I am optimistic about the future." *(The possibilities are endless.)*

"Everybody else is doing it, I am going to, too!" *(I need to be up there with the best.)*

'You've got to have some fun before you die!" *(Live now, pay later.)*

"Everything has a risk. You have to try it out." *(Yes I'm scared but I need to know.)*

"Let's take advantage of the situation before someone else does!" *(We need to be first.)*

"We are in this together!" *(There's no turning back.)*

"I'll go first, you follow." *(I'll show you how good I am.)*

"I am going to impress them!" *(You will take notice.)*

"I've got the latest one…" *(I never come away empty handed.)*

"Don't tell me you're still hanging on to that old stuff?" *(You're old fashioned.)*

When these two 'characters' combine they can have complementary and contradictory affects on our personality. Our Warrior can be a social opportunist and attempt to establish interest to gain status, which can extend from business to social partnerships and may even exhibit a sexual appetite. In all these relationships, the Servant moderates the behaviour of the Warrior, keeping it within social boundaries.

Scenario: How a person acting from their Warrior/Servant uses bantering to diffuse tension

> Stacey and his friends are having a beer and talking football. During the course of the conversation, one friend becomes upset with the other, as the jokes turn personal. Stacey intervenes when the two friends are near to blows. Stacey interjects cheerfully, 'Chill out! We came here to have fun, not to punch each other out!'

Stacey's Warrior/Servant steps in to lighten up a tense situation between friends that could even lead to physical violence. This scenario illustrates that a small degree of the Servant's influence on the Warrior can change social situations. The Servant makes Stacey intervene and diffuse the tension.

The Servant/Warrior
Build commitment and intimacy

If we are influenced mainly by these two 'characters' we convey a drive for physical and emotional intimacy, with emphases on gaining confidence and sharing personal and common interests to gain a sense of security within the relationship. The Servant brings the need for intimacy, the Warrior brings the determination to gain it. The desire in a relationship is to be considered as equal to the other. Servant/Warriors seek loyalty and weigh the relationship's benefit against the negatives to work towards finding a balance.

In this synergy the Servant is still supportive, but the focus is no longer about satisfying other's needs without question. In the supporting role, the Warrior brings to the relationship assertive acquisitiveness and mental resourcefulness. The Warrior's assertive qualities enhance the qualities of the Servant, seeking physical and emotional intimacy through gaining reassurance and confirmation that builds trust. In childhood this is seen when a child helps a parent in some form of problem-solving activity, or in general in helping roles building intimacy.

The Servant/Warrior is empathetic while at the same time cautious, and uses an evaluative and questioning approach before making a commitment. Servant/Warriors generally do not make decisions without knowing what is expected of them, and will ensure there are common interests on which to build trust. They can be powerful social crusaders, using reason and intellect to motivate others to join them. They have a need to improve the world. They will associate with people who boost their sense of security. It is their good nature that attracts others to them. They form emotional and intellectual relationships.

If an individual expresses the negative qualities of the Servant/Warrior she or he takes life too seriously and tends to be concerned with details, not the whole story. If rejected by an individual or group, the Servant/Warrior may wonder *"Why did this happen to me?"* When things go wrong Servant/Warriors tend to brood on what they could have done. They will compare and discuss the social status of people relative to themselves, emphasizing negative comparisons. If they feel they have been sidelined, envy may rear its head.

'Servant/Warrior' type personalities can be mildly introverted, but still enjoy intellectual pursuits. They are cautious in social environments, and require time to deliberate before making decisions. In personal relationships they prefer a mutual approach to solving problems. Group sports are often an important aspect of their nature as kinship with others helps validate their sense of identity. They consolidate relationships by building trust, testing emotional and mental compatibility and commitment, as they are nest-builders at heart.

The signature of these 'characters' in synergy is a calming and encouraging tone. They will have a detailed leaning approach to problem solving and have a diligent work ethic. They are socially modest, tactful, passionate, idealistic, and can be self-conscious when praised. They use humour in a self-deprecating manner and can exhibit a strong social conscience. They are found in occupations where there is personal contact and the opportunity to deal with emotional, mental and physical issues in a practical way. They lean towards 'people-centred' problem-solving activities.

Occupations of people with this 'character' synergy are often in industries such as health and education, research and environmental activities, journalism or writing, physical coaching or therapy, technical or engineering, liaison work or vocational counselling or psychology; they may be rights activists and engage in animal/humanitarian organisations. Other occupational areas could include being an inventor, architectural vocations or working as a personal assistant.

Servant/Warrior's underlying intention in communication is to build trust and gain commitment:

"We have to do something to help." *(I need support in this issue.)*
"It's wrong for us not to be involved." *(We have a responsibility.)*
"Let's do it together!" *(You build my confidence.)*
"If I do this for you, will you do… for me?" *(I want to know if I can rely on you.)*
"I can do it if you join me." *(I need to know I can trust you.)*
"I am not too sure it is what I want to do." *(I need to weigh up the consequences.)*
"There are so many choices; I am confused." *(I would like them all.)*
"How do I know you won't change your mind?" *(I need reassurance.)*
"I want to discuss making changes in our relationship." *(I am not sure about the direction we are going.)*

Scenario: A person acting from their Servant/Warrior would come to supporting a friend

James has been blamed for a mistake that his friend Ryan made and Ryan finds out about it. Ryan goes to see his employer and owns up to making the mistake. He also points out that further inquiries could have been made before someone was wrongly blamed.

*Ryan's Servant/Warrior demonstrates his commitment
to the friendship by acting to correct the injustice.*

Warrior/Servant and Servant/Warrior personalities form the tribal relationship

The Warrior/Servant synergy brings the capacity to acquire material resources for the physical benefit of the people in the relationship and the Servant/Warrior brings an ability to engender emotional intimacy necessary for bonding. When two people in a social encounter engage in testing the bases on which to build a relationship, one may express their Warrior/Servant and the other person their Servant/Warrior. If they bring together their mutual interests and an understanding is reached, a relationship can be formed. On an intellectual level, it is necessary to find compatibility through common interests and there is flexibility in these early stages of the relationship. Warrior/Servant and Servant/Warrior personalities have different perspectives on problem solving. They seek a solution in an entirely different manner from each other. A Warrior/Servant will see things from a strictly material perspective. *'If we buy this product or that accessory, we will be happier and the problem will be solved.'* The Servant/Warrior, on the other hand, will consider the effect on the relationship, *'I would like us to discuss the proposed purchase more fully. I don't want either of us to have any regrets afterwards.'*

A culture is formed when patterns of behaviour start to become ritualised. Once rituals become formalised it indicates that the Chief is starting to have a dominant influence in the relationship. This is where the relationship forms a culture where expectation starts to take shape. For example, a person expressing a Warrior/Servant synergy encourages the other in a relationship to take time out, while showing some degree of empathy. A person expressing Servant/Warrior synergy will say they have to complete the task before having recreational time. It also shows the different perspectives in the way they deal with problems that impact their relationship.

The Chief/Servant

Maintain the structure of the culture

In the Chief/Servant synergy, in which the Chief is the dominant 'character', leadership is conveyed through an even-handed administration of power, to establish values that strengthen the group's cohesion by focusing on the whole group's interest. We do this by delegating, using a reasoned approach. It is important to show fairness and acknowledge that everyone brings something to the table, even if they don't call the shots. We consider the intellectual abilities of each member of the group, their physical and emotional needs, and how these fit with the roles they are expected to play in ensuring the group's identity. We will be prepared to accept responsibility when mistakes have been made by talking through the issues to reach a group resolution. The contribution of others is valued, provided they act in the group's interest and support the need to find consensus.

In this synergy the Chief has authority to make decisions and the Servant gives the relationship the ability to listen and to make emotional connections. This amalgam of attributes gives the capacity to express reason, to make sense of the situation, supported by facts, to establish group co-operation while maintaining the integrity of individuals and the tribe. The executive function enhances our relationships by building commitment and loyalty into routines and processes within the group. This co-operative approach creates a positive outcome and promotes group spirit. This synergy also becomes active in situations that require the overcoming of a strong habitual response or resisting temptation.

The negative aspect of the Chief/Servant synergy, when responding to external threats, is it may be necessary to sacrifice the least important asset for the good of the group. This could be a person and not a material asset. At times, it may be possible to operate within acceptable social frameworks. However, it may be necessary to step outside what are perceived as normal ethical boundaries to maintain the integrity of the group. This is when the 'Primitive Chief' might come into play.

Chief/Servant type personalities are found in leadership roles, where planning, delegating and organisation skills are required or where arbitration is required between individuals and within organisations. Chief/Servants are prudent in the use of resources and in defining boundaries. They allocate roles and set realistic goals to encourage others to act in a constructive way, with the expectation of a beneficial outcome.

The signature of these 'characters' in synergy in an individual is the encouragement of co-operation, negotiation to maintain the group's culture and the use of questioning such as, *"Give me a reason for this"*, *"What is the logic behind this?"* and *"How can I support you in what needs to be done?"* Chief/Servants will use eye contact and a strong and reassuring tone of voice.

People with this 'character' synergy are often found working in industries such as psychology and administration or as consultants of some description or as a senior police/military officer or a school principal. Other occupational areas could include an accounts manager or judge, human resource manager or senior medical manager, university lecturer or solicitor. This 'character' is often found in senior ranks within any of these types of occupations.

The Chief/Servant's underlying intention in communication is to encourage cooperation through leadership:

"These are the instructions, follow them", "If things do not work out the way I anticipate, then I will review them." *(I am prepared to make changes from your feedback.)*

"Before anything is done I must consider the ramifications for the group/tribe." *(I am not going to put the relationships at risk.)*

"I have to consider what I feel about the issue." *(I need to explore all aspects.)*

"We have to be prepared to make changes in our approach within some *restrictions.*" *(I need to have limits that I feel I can manage.)*

"We are in this together." *(I need you to know I expect you to support me.)*

"Try it out for yourself." "If you find it difficult to get back to me." *(I am willing to give you the opportunity to show me I can trust you.)*

"I appreciate the hard work you have done." *(You have made me feel good.)*

'You've really done a good job." *(I'd like you to continue doing a good job.)*

"You handled a difficult situation very well." *(I admire you.)*

Scenario: How a person acting from a Chief/Servant synergy would deal with an accident.

Jim sees an accident has taken place at the intersection: two vehicles have collided. An adult and three children emerge from one car and are shaken by the experience. In the other vehicle the driver seems all right. People start to gather around the accident scene and Jim firmly asks someone to phone the ambulance and police and sends someone for help. He then asks if someone has first aid skills and gets them to attend to the casualties. He then organises someone to alert other motorists of the hazards.

Jim's Chief/Servant is activated as he deals with the situation from a safety and organisational perspective. By prioritising and instructing others to act, he brings the situation under control.

Servant/Chief
Maintain the morals and values of the culture

In the Servant/Chief synergy the Servant is the dominant 'character'. Servant/Chiefs convey a willingness to take care of others in a personal context, encouraging compliance, service, and emotional connection. This is achieved through nurturing and teaching of family/group values. This is seen in parent-child and teacher-pupil relationships. In organisations, individuals expressing this synergy would be beneficial in the building of morale.

In this synergy the Servant's focus is for emotional connection and maintaining intimacy, whereas the Chief defines personal boundaries and organises the way they are maintained. This amalgam of attributes gives the capacity to build rapport, trust and reliability. This set of skills enhances relationships with interpersonal communication building, which strengthens cultural ties by promoting routines connected with obligation and respect for the values of the group. These interpersonal bonds encourage conformity to customs of the group. This participatory approach fosters emotional and physical dependency, which strengthens a sense of security and belonging. Servant/Chiefs build and maintain civil and social boundaries on a personal level by teaching, encouraging and participating in forming emotional dependency in each generation, so people are obligated to act in the interests of the tribe. This is expressed in a paternal approach that promotes the essential 'tribal glue' that establishes the ritualistic behaviour to form routines necessary in the process of maintaining tribal interests.

The negative reaction of Servant/Chiefs to external threats is over-protective. Anxiety and insecurity may also cause them to defend the indefensible. For instance, if someone with whom they have little emotional connection criticises their family or friends they may defend them even if they know the accusations are true. They encourage others to be dependent on them in order to build obligation. They can play favourites to maintain a dependency and often make judgments about others that are based on fears and prejudice.

Servant/Chief type personalities promote obligation through emotional attachment. In cases of conflict within their group they are good conciliators. They are loyal to those they feel responsible for and sometimes can be unnecessarily self-sacrificing. They bring a personal touch into strengthening emotional and physical belonging, which contributes to maintaining social networks. They often work behind the scenes in getting things done. They encourage and maintain group cultural values with a sense of unity and commitment. This is achieved by forming emotional and physical bonds to develop a sense of belonging and obligation. They use words that are affirming, encouraging and use physical contact to build emotional attachment.

The signature of these 'characters' in synergy in an individual is behaviour that acts to sustain physical bonds and promote group unity. The Servant/Chief is empathetic, protective, encourages participation, is supportive in an emotional and physical nurturing way and can be very moralistic.

Occupations of people with this ''character' synergy are often found in industries that involve emotional support and physical support and the need to maintain interpersonal relationships, such as pre-school teachers or special needs teachers, receptionists or human resources workers, social workers, disability workers or nurses, age-care workers or 'general' community care workers.

The Servant/Chief's underlying intention in communication is to build emotional bonds through fostering cultural values:

"Let me show you how to do that..." *(I realise that it could be difficult.)*

"If you do it this way it will work." *(I will show you the way it should be done.)*

"I know you are upset. It will be all right now I am here." *(I can defend you.)*

"Let's try it out." *(I want you to learn.)*

"Let's look at the positives of this situation." *(I want you to be comforted by words.)*

'I don't like you play near the road." *(I feel vulnerable, without control.)*

"Don't accuse my child of doing wrong!" *(You attack my child you attack me.)*

"I know you could not help it." *(I am prepared to accept it was not intentional.)*

"I bet that was painful." "Let me look at it." *(You need me help you.)*

"We are family; your problem is my problem." *(You are not alone.)*

"I will be here for you when you need me." *(You can always depend on me.)*

Scenario: how a person acts through their Servant/Chief when setting boundaries

Barbara's son Larry is working on his bike in the tool shed, which he usually leaves a mess. Barbara grumbles about the state of the garage each time but cleans up each time. This time however, when Larry finishes working on the bike, she says:
'The shed is in a bit of a mess, let's clean it up together.'

They clean up the garage and then Barbara says:
'I would appreciate the garage being left clean like this in the future.'

Barbara's Servant/Chief is emotionally supportive and participatory in order to educate her son into clean work practices. This could prevent any future conflict on this issue.
The Chief/Servant will want to know what effects an activity will have on the tribe, whereas the Servant/Chief is more concerned about the safety of an activity on a personal level.

When taking a problem to a Chief/Servant type, expect to be questioned about your competency to solve the problem. They may suggest time be spent looking at options. They will expect you to find results from self-motivation. The Servant/Chief type will coach the person with a problem, supporting and encouraging them by participating in finding a solution. The interlinking between the Chief/Servant's and the Servant/Chief's interests allows consideration of both individual and organisational needs.

The Chief in synergy with the Servant plays a central role in influencing the operational structure of the tribe. As such, the Chief/Servant is the tribal manager and the Servant/Chief is the supervisor. Both are equally important and have equal influence in the way the tribal culture develops. This in turn has an important function in defining the roles we play within our social groups that maintain a balance within the culture.

Within the nature of the Chief and Servant synergy there is cultural memory and wisdom, which is linked to the present; and a focus on the importance of kinship through emotional ties. They build tribal memory and cultural values that are passed from one generation to another. When these two 'characters' act in synergy they ensure the maintenance of customs, which in turn sustains the values of the culture.

The dialogue that we express in synergistic transactions can produce varied responses from the different sets of 'characters'. In this we show the synergistic 'characters' interactions we may be familiar with. If, for example, a person who has responsibility for others expresses their Chief/Servant, they will use an encouraging tone to bring about cooperation. This could elicit several responses, such as the person they are addressing responding from their Warrior/Servant, saying, *"This is not a problem!"* They will want to impress, showing an individualistic approach to getting things done. Whereas the Servant/Warrior will be cautious, asking, *"What will this entail?"* They will want to know what is required of them before they feel they can do what is requested. The Servant/Chief will be supportive, *"I will lend a hand when it's needed."* They supervise, keeping the group on task. The Mentor role helps to achieve a fair and realistic outcome if conflicts occur.

This diagam illustrates the different reaction to a leader who encouraging cooperation between staff members.

Diagram of traits of 'characters' in synergy

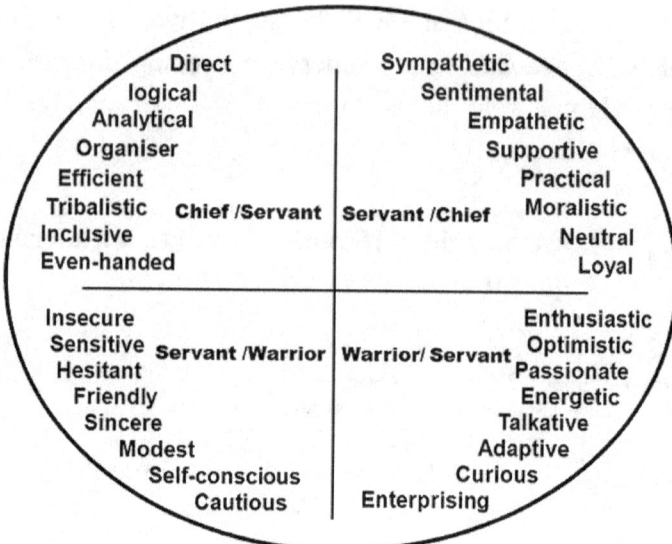

Warrior/Servant - explores the potential for relationships
Servant/ Warrior – builds trust and commitment in a relationship
Chief/Servant – manages the arrangements within a relationship
Servant/Chief – strengthens and maintains emotional bonds.

The Tribal Mentor

The difference between the Personal Mentor and the tribal Mentor is that the personal mentor deals with your own conscience regarding others on a personal level, acting from a view that influences self (any action where we are judging our *own* values or behaviours). The Tribal Mentor acts from a view that influences the group and the relationship in the context of the wider world. Tribal Mentors usually deal with issues that involve helping others to resolve misunderstandings or a conflict situation, acting impartially on behalf of each antagonist. The

Tribal Mentor is patient and tolerant, believing in the intrinsic intelligence of others to appropriately deal with their problems. He or she enables others to find their own solutions to contentious issues. They consider diplomacy and the promotion of self-awareness to be essential for the resolution of problems. The communication style of the Mentor will be focused on validating and enabling others to remain independent by evoking their own understanding, knowledge and ability to resolve their problems.

When our Tribal Mentor is dominant our emotional intellect is awakened. We also become aware of our interdependence and the impact we are able to exert on others and of their influence on us. This enables us to take responsibility for our communication, decisions and actions and to seek honesty and to act impartially. We also become aware of our place in the world and we nurture a disinterested perspective on the human condition. We are aware of the suffering of others beyond our personal and tribal interests and want to alleviate it. We also encourage others to act with compassion both inside and outside the tribe. *Tribal Mentorship can be attributed to the elders of a group.* Acting from this 'character' we will respond calmly, supportively, logically and ethically. Tribal Mentors use knowledge that is within the synergy of the other 'characters' to bring an inclusive perspective into play. They have a great understanding of others' feelings, a generosity of spirit, independence of thought and clear-minded purpose.

When our Tribal Mentor connects with our Chief and Warrior through the Servant, their unique qualities become a powerful agent for change in consciousness. Our Chief brings understanding of the organisation and administration of the tribe; our Warrior contributes dynamic energy, adaptability and creativity; our Servant adds a sense of service and connection to others. Our Tribal Mentor integrates these qualities and this allows us to operate with greater perspective and foresight. When dealing with ethical issues a person expressing the Mentor will be guided by the need to 'cause no harm and considering the practical, emotional and ethical consequences of an action.

If our Mentor is actively engaged with our other 'characters' in a quest to find answers to problems, we may experience moments of great insight. This happens because we are motivated by all levels of our consciousness, applying the Mentor as catalyst in bringing all the 'characters' together to achieve one objective. There is no fragmentation of the self; the 'characters' act in concert as one self, free from our own or other restrictions and prejudices. When we apply the qualities of our Mentor we are able to achieve a complete sense of our own reality.

The Mentor appeals to the higher nature of others in times of conflict. The Mentor gathers all the facts before forming an opinion. In acting from this 'character' we may sometimes put our personal safety at risk in order to support others. In a physical and verbal attack, if the situation is irrational, the Mentor 'character' has very little influence. It is only when the energy in a conflict has dissipated, and mental reasoning and emotional sense of balance is restored, that the Mentor can have any influence.

Who is a Mentor?

A Mentor's qualities may be seen in counsellors, friends, and people who facilitate in conflict situations that need a humanitarian as well as a practical answer. Statesmen, peace workers, social workers, arbitrators, ambassadors require independence of mind and the capacities of the Mentor.

False Mentor

A false Mentor plays the role of a Wise Sage and, as such, they maintain a distance from others. They operate apart from the very people they claim to help. This adaptive state may be the result of childhood experiences of high expectations, where the emphasis was on the necessity to *be nice* or to *gain praise* to avoid conflict. In adults, this state is expressed as a way of avoiding exposing the vulnerability and fears that underlie a sense of superiority. This divorces people from their own feelings and prevents their gaining intimacy with others.

False Mentors use the problems of others to escape facing their own issues by promoting an image of being always supremely calm and constantly dispensing advice. They use helping roles to encourage others to become dependent on them and use a variety of persuasive tactics to support of their own agenda. They mask their real personality in Mentor roles: the other 'characters' may be lurking below the surface. The Warrior may masquerade as a Mentor to gain power or the Chief may do so to consolidate power. If we act predominantly from either of these 'characters' in a relationship, we will prevent intimacy.

Discovering your personality 'character' type questionnaire

The Questionnaire below is designed to give a general indication of the 'characters' that play a strong part in your behaviour. For each of the traits listed below, write in the appropriate box a number as it applies to you, using the following 1 to 5 scale: **1 = Never. 2 = Seldom. 3 = Sometimes. 4 = Often. 5 = Most of the time.**

Write the number in the box beside the trait. Add the numbers in each column to get the total for that group. At the bottom of the questionnaire is information about which 'characters' traits are indicated in the columns.

1
- ☐ Rebellious
- ☐ Manipulative
- ☐ Competitive
- ☐ Unpredictable
- ☐ Spiteful
- ☐ Acquisitive
- ☐ Devious
- ☐ Exploitive
- ☐ Total

2
- ☐ Defensive
- ☐ Territorial
- ☐ Rigid
- ☐ Controlling
- ☐ Pessimistic
- ☐ Critical
- ☐ Demanding
- ☐ Opinionated
- ☐ Total

3
- ☐ Compliant
- ☐ Careful
- ☐ Pleasing
- ☐ Helpful
- ☐ Vulnerable
- ☐ Reliable
- ☐ Trusting
- ☐ Anxious
- ☐ Total

4
- ☐ Authentic
- ☐ Objective
- ☐ Impartial
- ☐ Ethical
- ☐ Conscientious
- ☐ Prudent
- ☐ Composed
- ☐ Altruistic
- ☐ Total

5
- ☐ Direct
- ☐ logical
- ☐ Analytical
- ☐ Organised
- ☐ Efficient
- ☐ Tribalistic
- ☐ Inclusive
- ☐ Even-handed
- ☐ Total

6
- ☐ Sympathetic
- ☐ Sentimental
- ☐ Empathetic
- ☐ Supportive
- ☐ Practical
- ☐ Moralistic
- ☐ Nurturing
- ☐ Loyal
- ☐ Total

7
- ☐ Insecure
- ☐ Self-conscious
- ☐ Hesitant
- ☐ Friendly
- ☐ Questioning
- ☐ Modest
- ☐ Sincere
- ☐ Cautious
- ☐ Total

8
- ☐ Enthusiastic
- ☐ Adventurous
- ☐ Passionate
- ☐ Energetic
- ☐ Optimistic
- ☐ Talkative
- ☐ Adaptive
- ☐ Curious
- ☐ Total

9
- ☐ Courteous
- ☐ Attentive
- ☐ Receptive
- ☐ Reflective
- ☐ Inquisitive
- ☐ Patient
- ☐ Objective
- ☐ Compassionate
- ☐ Total

10
- ☐ Resentful
- ☐ Discontented
- ☐ Schemer
- ☐ Evasive
- ☐ Resistant
- ☐ Disloyal
- ☐ Detached
- ☐ Martyring
- ☐ Total

11
- ☐ Obedient
- ☐ Abused
- ☐ Helpless
- ☐ Self-Deprecating
- ☐ Withdrawn
- ☐ Depressed
- ☐ Anxious
- ☐ Apprehensive
- ☐ Total

Relationships of convenience: Warrior and Chief

A relationship of convenience is one that is devoid of morality and ethics. In this type of relationship there is little or no emotional connection or regard by one individual for the other, as every transaction is seen as having the potential to advantage self-interest. This type of relationship can often be seen in business transactions and employee/employer relationships.

A relationship of convenience is an alliance between Primitive 'characters' in which both parties intend to gain from the situation and *there is no synergistic relationship whatsoever*. The Warrior will act on behalf of the Chief solely to gain rewards, and the Chief will use the Warrior solely to maintain power. This relationship has a corrupt and sometimes an illegal nature. There is also a high degree of intrigue because the Chief and Warrior seek only to serve self-interest. This is achieved by professing loyalty and conveying an impression of co-operation, whilst at the same time advancing their own interests.

Any relationship that is based solely on gain has the potential to develop into a situation where someone can become disadvantaged emotionally, financially, mentally and physically, or made a scapegoat if things go wrong. In such a scenario, either party may turn into a Slave.

In this relationship the Primitive Chief type will strive to maintain status and dominion over what she or he considers are her or his possessions, and will have no sentiment or loyalty to others. The relationship is based solely on convenience, without humanity, with the intention of retaining what people have and what they think should belong to them. The Warrior uses people to gain material status. Warriors may imply willingness to help maintain the status of another, while they are only interested in enhancing their own. If they reach a state of confidence and feel they can challenge the other person's position, they will dethrone them without sentiment to become the Chief. Both 'characters' work to ensure their survival and in a premeditated way. Without the transforming influence of the Servant, the Chief and Warrior will exploit each other's weakness to the maximum, using unethical practices to gain an advantage. The reason for these two opposing interests forming a relationship, however temporary, is in order to gain what they need. This relationship of convenience necessitates mercenary or Machiavellian behaviour. If you read history you will find many references to this type of behaviour, such as those of English Kings, Barons and Knights using each other for their own ends. Whenever the Primitive 'characters' are intensely active in a relationship there is the possibility for conflict. When this happens, territory, status and relationships can be lost or gained.

Scenarios: Relationships of convenience

1. John was using his own time to run the department while Harry, his manager, was offloading his own responsibility onto John so that he could freelance for extra money during regular working hours. John took on extra responsibility in addition to his own job with no personal recognition or financial benefit.
Finally fed up, John decides to supplement his salary by taking company goods home. He also told Harry that with all the additional work he expected a raise in salary, and that if the raise wasn't forthcoming he was thinking of looking for another job. John knew that this would put Harry in a difficult position, as Harry's moonlighting activities would have to cease.

Harry agreed that John should be rewarded for his hard work. However, he also informed John that he was investigating 'stock loss' and it would be a shame if people risked their present and future job prospects because of petty pilfering. He ended the conversation by telling John that, with his excellent organisational skills, he would be missed if he had to leave.

Harry and John, in exploiting the company for their own ends, have reached a stalemate. Their corrupt deception has created a situation where each is unable to take action against the other without damaging their own reputation. They both have a limited degree of power to manipulate each other, and are vulnerable to conflict. We see a 'character' shift in both John (Servant to Warrior) and Harry (Chief to Warrior). The stand-off is difficult to resolve.

2. Jill's landlord advises her he will not be renewing her lease as he has decided to sell the house. She decides to look for new accommodation.

Her search turns up nothing, and just as she begins to panic, Jonathan, whom she knows casually and doesn't particularly like, approaches her. He offers her space in his house. She could move in immediately, and the rent would be moderate in exchange for house cleaning and meal preparation.

Jill accepts the offer, despite her discomfort at sharing space with Jonathon, let alone cleaning and cooking for him. She decides she would put up with the situation until she finds another place and is able to move out as soon as possible.

Under stress, Jill is powerless and vulnerable (Slave). Wanting a quick resolution to her problem, she puts aside her feelings towards Jonathan and his terms, until she can find something better (Warrior). Jonathan, an opportunist, is pleased to have someone to organise and maintain his territory on his terms (Chief).

The intertwining of self-interest with the tribe's interest

There are many times in a person's life when there is a conflict of interest between personal needs and the needs of others. In order to gain greater security, we will weigh up the degree of compromise we are prepared to make to maintain the relationship by adapting our *principle* needs.

Here is an example to illustrate this point. A researcher is faced with solving a problem that could benefit society while at the same time gaining the researcher money and status. The researcher's motivation may be to help the group, to help the researcher himself or herself, or both. The researcher may act on his or her Servant/Warrior needs to serve the interest of the group, or may act ruthlessly to gain the answers to the problem with no regard other than to profit self. That can still produce a reasoned and prudent response to an issue that benefits the researcher and others. This example can be applied to many decision-making situations.

You may have faced circumstances where you have had to consider your personal interest against that of others. What 'characters' do you feel where in involved in your decisions?

The following scenario shows how the same kind of synergy influences the way two people interact, based upon their own needs and values.

Scenario: Giving a helping hand

> Benjamin, an elderly man, planted potatoes in his garden but when his bountiful harvest was ready he was not well enough to dig them up. John, his next-door neighbour, noticed his plight and dug them up for him. A week later John was preparing a surprise dinner for his wife and discovered they had run out of potatoes. He asked Benjamin if he could have a few potatoes.

Benjamin's response will indicate the degree of 'character' synergy within the transaction. He may respond by saying, "No! I cannot afford to give you any", acting from his Primitive Chief, in which case there is no synergy at all. He may be begrudging in his response, "Here's a few. I expect you to return the favour." In this response Benjamin is acting from his Primitive Warrior. He wants make John feel indebted. He may say, "I'll get you a few, give me them back when you can." This response demonstrates a degree of synergy – the Servant has influenced the Chief somewhat, and Benjamin is willing to share a limited quantity. Finally, "There's a sack over there, help yourself." This response, a decision to share generously with John, tells us Benjamin's 'characters' are in synergy . It is the degree of obligation that determines our response.

Identifying 'character' responses:

Any one situation will engender a particular 'character' response. Depending on the circumstances and 'character' predisposition, you may respond with one or more of the 'characters' we have discussed. Read the following situation and see what 'characters' you are likely to express.

Scenario: Avoiding responsibility

> Colin obtains a new job as Department Head. The Department, however, is a low priority in the company and does not get the attention or assets Colin needs in order to carry out his job effectively. Colin must rely on Duncan, one of his staff members, who has a great deal of knowledge and experience in the department. Duncan supports Colin from the beginning. The running of an under-staffed, under-resourced department, along with the reliance on a subordinate Duncan, causes Colin undue stress. After a particularly stressful meeting with his boss, Colin calls in Duncan and accuses him of not giving him enough support.

Duncan's response could be:

(Warrior) *Colin! Get stuffed, I'm not doing any more than I am paid to do!*

(Chief) *Start sorting out your own job before you start sorting out my job!*

(Servant) *I'm sorry if I've caused any problems; what can I do to put things right?*

(Servant/Warrior)

Colin, can we discuss what areas you would like me to be responsible for so I can do my job right?

(Mentor) *I know it's been a difficult time for you. I would like to find a more beneficial way for both of us.*

76

(Slave) *Nods Walk away; feel so overwhelmed he has no response*

(Warrior/Servant) *Come on, Colin, get a life! I have enough on my plate; I don't need any more 'laughs'!*

(Chief/Servant) *I think this department needs better administration, so we can see how to delegate responsibilities.*

(Servant/Chief) *I may need more support in supervision of the staff for better delivery of our tasks.*

(Tribal Mentor) *I need to support Colin by convening a meeting with other staff members, to tell them I am going to be more involved in finding a resolution to the high workload problem.*

(Recalcitrant Slave) *I have had enough of this job, I am going to make it difficult for them!* 'Management'

Motives behind 'character' dialogue

'Characters' express motives and intent that communicate our needs and determine the direction our relationships take. When we meet people we may engage in dialogue that defines territory, status, common interests and security. The 'character' being expressed can usually be detected by the words chosen, tone of voice, facial expression and body gestures. The underlying intent behind any communication will influence the conversation's direction and may generate a negative, neutral or positive response. As we discover more about the person we are conversing with, the relationship may change the 'characters' we express.

We have all experienced and expressed some of these behaviours. The way someone approaches us or the way we approach them will indicate the 'characters' involved. But assumptions and expectations also play an important part in influencing how we listen to ourselves and other people. If we listen carefully, we will understand the 'characters' influencing the communication.

Our interpretation of any given transaction is influenced by the vulnerabilities and strengths of our own particular 'characters'.

Understanding the way we lead into a conversation – the words we use and what we think or our intention – will help us define the 'characters' at work in our behaviour. Following is a list of comments that are commonly used when we meet people for the first time. The expressions can be used deliberately or unconsciously to define territory, status, influence, common interests, and security.

Tick the boxes that apply to your approach and think which of your 'characters' are involved:

☐ 'Good to finally meet you!'

☐ 'How long have you known Carol, our hostess?'

☐ 'I see you still have that old car!'

☐ 'Where do you live?'

☐ 'I'm new to the area and haven't had time to get to know anyone yet!'

☐ 'What kind of work do you do?'

☐ 'Have you been with the company long?'

☐ 'I saw you at the Warrington Club. Are you a member?'

☐ 'I'm into sports and movies. What are your interests?

☐ 'I see you are one of us.'

☐ 'I hear you are on the opposing side!'

☐ 'Doesn't the food look inviting?'

☐ 'Hello. Great party! Have you known Pat long?'

☐ 'Isn't this a lovely setting for a party?'

☐ 'I went to Burkdale College where I got an honours degree in science. What college did you go to?"

☐ 'I know Jack Simons; he's an old friend of mine. He may be able to help you.'

☐ 'Hi. What's your connection with this event?'

☐ 'I bet this party was expensive!'

☐ 'I work at Parker & Co as a draftsman. What do you do for a living?

☐ 'Nice to meet you; I've heard a lot about you.'

You may have other ways of engaging others; see if you can identify the 'character'.

In the conversation starters listed above, tick the boxes you can identify personally and consider the following questions below.

Which of the comments (including similar comments) are you likely to make? _____

_____

_____

Were you able to identify the 'character' with a particular approach? _____

_____

_____

The underlying intent behind your communication is to?

_____

_____

_____

Which of the various greetings evoked strong feeling in you?

_____

_____

_____

A 'character's' communication style

The style of our communication will reflect which of our 'characters' is involved. If people are influenced by their Chief, they will compare territory and status; if their Warrior is engaged they will seek attention by boasting about their achievements; if the Servant is expressed they will search for security through common interests; if the Mentor is dominant they will communicate sociably with no hidden agenda and avoiding strong opinions.

Conversation starters set the climate in our communication with others. This can change as we discover more about the other person, but the conversation starters can set the tone – and it can sometimes be very difficult to change first impressions.

Awareness of our 'characters' and the 'characters' in others will help us to see conversational styles more clearly – both our own and those of others. Recognising the different styles through which 'characters' communicate – and their impact – may help us become more flexible in the dialogue we use and help us to change our delivery and response, as desired. In some social situations dynamics can change very quickly and we can be surprised by the way events unfold. Think of the situations you have experienced and the 'characters' that were in play at that time.

The scenario below shows how social encounters can bring disconcerting and surprising outcomes.

Scenario: Exploring relationships

Steven is invited to a friend's party. He is one of the first to arrive. He watches people coming into the room hoping to see some familiar faces but his busy hosts appear to be the only people he knows.

He finally approaches two people who seem to be as out-of-place as he feels.

'Hi, my name is Steven.'

They introduce themselves as Michael and Andrew. He discovers that he and Andrew are neighbours. Not only that, but it turns out that Steven worked at the same engineering firm where Andrew works. During the course of the conversation, Steven and Andrew find they have a lot in common. Michael excuses himself and moves away.

Then Andrew mentions his best friend. Steven, it turns out, has had major conflicts with this person. The atmosphere becomes tense, and Steven excuses himself.

This situation illustrates the way we use questions to explore and test boundaries in a search for safety, and sociability, or to gain advantage. It shows how we affect people by including or excluding them in the topics we cover. It also demonstrates how we compare status and define territory. Finally, it shows the indirect effect of a third party (someone who is not present or not included in the conversation) on a relationship.

When we encounter disconcerting social transactions, it is usually because there has been an unexpected switch in 'characters'. This often occurs spontaneously. When we are deep in conversation we tend to focus on the part of the transaction that relates to our interests. That is why it is hard to read the cue denoting a switch in 'characters'. There are two types of transactions. Primitive transactions negate the interests of others. Most of us have experienced a switch to the Primitives when we feel threatened. Then there is the synergistic 'character' response, which considers others as well as oneself. There are many instances when we may shift our approach to make others feel comfortable. We may be at a social function where there are multiple conversational transactions in which switches in 'character' are required to maintain sociability. We have to be mindful that our Primitive nature can emerge when strong emotions are being expressed in a transaction. You may have noticed switches in your own behaviours, particularly when meeting strangers. We can misrepresent ourselves due to vulnerability.

Scenario: Switching 'character'

Imagine you are in a restaurant having coffee with a friend. Someone your friend knows sits down at the next table and the two of them start talking. You notice your friend's manner has changed. Instead of her usual tendency to be bossy and opinionated, she has become more restrained, attentive and agreeable.

When the other person leaves, your friend informs you that person was the president of the new club she has joined.

You have just witnessed a switch, in 'character' from Chief to Servant. When one of our 'characters' increases in intensity another of our 'characters' may decrease and this can limit our ability to see things in their true perspective (an exception to this would be our Mentor, if fully developed).

Our range of communication includes everything from shouting to whispering, and all the accompanying gestures and postures. Silence is also a form of communication and can infer defiance (Warrior), displeasure or indifference (Chief), acquiescence (Servant), support (Mentor) or disobedience (a Slave).

Our style of communicating ultimately affects our relationships in some form. How it does so will depend on the extent to which our 'characters' have developed internally. This will reflect on how we feel in a given situation. We may switch from one 'character' to another – we may be supportive one minute and defensive the next. Although we may not know exactly how a person will respond to what we say, the 'characters' they express will indicate their feelings about what we have communicated. For instance, you are usually a friendly, engaging, and co-operative person, but you may change that approach if you feel threatened. Have you ever been in a situation where a person you thought you would support suddenly presents ideas that were yours or gave information to others that was personal to you? This could cause you to drop your support, but you may also find yourself attacking that other person. What has happened here? It's possible that your position is threatened and you react in a manner that is contrary to your normal disposition. If there is a strong Primitive in our communication style we will be prone to anger: even vengefulness can occur where loyalties have been broken. This switch happens because of a change in relationship dynamics and perceived threats to personal interests or the interests of people with whom you identify.

Scenario: Disloyalty

David and Mark have been friends since school days. They now work in the same division of a local factory. After five years, Mark applies for a supervisory position, and David encourages him. Mark's application is successful, and he is now David's supervisor.

Busy in his new role, Mark socialises less with David but continues their daily lunches together, during which, among other things, Mark asks David technical questions to fill in his own knowledge gaps. David obliges but feels increasingly discontented.

Soon another department supervisor joins David and Mark for lunch. He and Mark mainly discussed management issues. David feels angry and used; he finds a way to excuse himself from the daily lunches.

This scenario demonstrates how self-interest sometimes overrides a relationship. Here, we see Mark expressing his Servant/Warrior then switching to his Primitive Warrior, exploiting his friend David and dismissing him to Slave status – even if not intentionally. David moves from being a helpful friend (Servant/Warrior) to feeling alienated (Slave).

The signature of 'characters'

We have examined the traits, roles and temperaments of the 'characters'. Now we will explore the signature of each 'character' or combination of 'characters', which carry our intentions (what we think and feel). These are reflected in the way we behave.

We have discussed already how a conscious awareness of our 'characters' helps us achieve a measured response to a situation and its possible outcome. Awareness of the signatures each of our 'characters' has helps us understand what types of people we are attracted to and why they are attracted to us.

Scenarios: Examples below show how two or more 'character' signatures can be experienced at the same time.

Scenario 1: Anger and confusion

> Pete comes home unexpectedly and finds Barry, his flatmate, in his bedroom rummaging through his personal possessions. He is furious, responding from his Primitive Chief; feelings brought about by this invasion of his privacy. He is also saddened, which is a reflection from his Servant/Warrior nature: Barry is his friend; there must be a good reason for his actions.

> Angry and confused by his competing emotions, Pete demands to know what is going on. Barry tells him he has lost his passport and, as his flight is in two days, he is desperately trying to find it. Pete's anger subsides when he realises what the situation is. Wanting to help, he responds from his Warrior/Servant. He says: 'If it's in the house we will find it – but we will start in your bedroom first!'

Scenario 2: Concern and punishment

> Jessica is alarmed and fearful when she sees her son fall off his bike. She is also hopping mad at him for not wearing his helmet. She runs to him and scoops him up in her arms, checks on his

injuries and reassures herself that he is all right. This is a response from her Servant/Chief. She also feels like smacking him severely for not wearing his helmet – feelings from her Primitive Chief.

Scenario 3: Anger and fear of reprisal

Pat returns from lunch and finds the paperwork for preparing this month's accounts on her desk. Robbie, her manager, is responsible for preparing the accounts but has left them for her to do.

Pat, frustrated by this additional pressure on her, feels like telling Robbie what he should do with the accounts – feelings coming from her Primitive Warrior. However, she complies reluctantly because she is concerned about what will happen if she doesn't. This response comes from Slave feelings of powerlessness.

We may sometimes find ourselves in situations where we feel pulled in different directions – what we would like to do versus what others want us to do, or what we think is expected. The above scenarios demonstrate how there can be two or more 'characters' (either Primitive or 'characters' synergy) involved in one scenario. We may respond, then immediately realise that our response is not appropriate. For example, in Pat's scenario above, she ended up on the losing end of the situation because of her Slave fears. We may also respond in a measured manner, still feeling the Primitive pressure, as was the case with Jessica.

Parenting communication styles

Where do 'characters' come into play in the way we parent our children? Firstly, we have to consider family history and the types of 'characters' we saw our parents play and the effect of that on the development of our own 'characters'. This can become evident in a number of parenting styles. Individuals that express the following characters; Primitive Chief they will be controlling and demanding, and will use shaming and physical punishment to gain compliance. In the Chief/Servant they encourage commitment; with the loss of commitment they will take away privileges in order to regain it. The Servant/Chief they use coaxing and can use emotional distancing to show disapproval in order to refocus attention on tasks. In the Servant/Warrior they use a more academic approach that tends to apply popular modern psychological methods. Such individuals have analysed their childhood and do not wish to repeat their parents' style of upbringing. If they express the Warrior/Servant they will apply a laissez-faire approach. Individual expressing the Warrior/Servants tend to think children should grow up with few restrictions. They avoid taking responsibility in parenting their children. Some parents use a combination of styles appropriate to the age and disposition of the child. Using mixed styles – authoritarian, permissive and uninvolved – can be counterproductive.

Let's take an example: Your child is pestering you. If you are predisposed to expressing the Servant/Chief, you will be susceptible to giving in to his or her desires. The Warrior in children learns that if they keep chipping away at the foundation of the castle the walls will come down. The most common scenarios where we witness this kind of pestering (and therefore the erosion of the Chief content in the synergy) are when parents take children into a supermarket. They become confronted by the demands of their children's Primitive Warrior's desire for booty. The approach some parents choose is to pacify the child, while feeling like a powerless Slave. On the other hand they may use physical punishment (Primitive Chief) or firmly inform their children of the consequences of continuing the disruptive behaviour, such as withdrawal of privileges (Chief/Servant). Flexibility is important in considering appropriate responses. Has your upbringing affected the way you use your 'characters' in parenting? What parenting style – autocratic, permissive, or passive – do you and your partner apply? Sometimes we can adopt our own parents' style.

Role models

Role models expressed by caregivers and extended family can be instilled in the attitudes of children and reflected in their sense of right and wrong. Positive role modelling in the early years, shown in the respect we give to others, gives important messages. This can encourage a strong building of synergy between the 'characters' within the child, which can have a positive influence for adulthood. The larger the family circle, the more opportunity children will have to observe and assimilate behaviour and attitudes from the many roles people play within their tribe. A child exposed to this kind of environment is more likely to emulate these qualities. There are also other forms of role models that can be taken from literature and films, from music, art, teachers and fellow students. Culture can also act as a role model in the way it expresses values to live by: about what is right and wrong, what is reflected in beliefs and traditions. All these early influences contribute to our adopting 'character' synergistic behaviours that form our identity within the broader human tribe. Good role models help children to aspire to be better than they are and to engage with others in a socially acceptable way. If there are few role models, the opportunity for children to develop 'character' synergy in their personality is reduced. A child exposed to few role models will experience feelings of alienation, which will affect her or his ability to deal with conflicts in a successful beneficial manner.

A child without positive role models and who has a sense of powerlessness in an abusive environment is left vulnerable in life to his or her own emotions as well as the negative attitudes of others. Such a child can also feel strongly victimized, causing depression. She or he experiences the Infantile Slave. Children with such an upbringing may resort to crime or anti-social behaviour as a way of expressing their resentments through their Primitive Warrior or Recalcitrant Slave. An abusive environment reduces children's capacity to develop 'character' synergy in their nature, which would help them use internal dialogue to look at issues from perspectives other than their own. It is the synergistic qualities of the 'characters' that help us play back past and present experiences and put them into emotional and intellectual context.

The prison system in many countries focuses on punishment, which is frequently a continuation of the environment prisoners have experienced throughout life. Individuals who are imprisoned frequently lack synergistic qualities. Confining such an individual with other people with a similar perspective on life can reinforce feelings of victimisation. This will strengthen the Infantile Slave, Recalcitrant Slave or Primitive Warrior as a way of coping with internal pain. Often in these situations positive role models will be rare. It is important to help these individuals to reach an understanding of why their 'characters' work for or against them. This will give them an awareness of the qualities of positive 'characters' in their nature and will help to teach them, through observation, about the synergistic 'characters' in action.

People who become our role models express the 'character' synergistic qualities of Chief/Servant (shown in leadership),

Mentor (the peace maker), Servant/Chief (the nurturer), Warrior/Servant (courage) and Servant/Warrior (social conscience). People who exhibit these qualities in front of children give them positive insights on how to behave in relationships. A strong family and extended families will help a child to observe a broad spectrum of 'characters' in play and from this they can witness examples of behaviours that build relationship as well as those that do not. Role models are not just a few individuals in a child's life, for example some people who may stand out because they show empathy and compassion. There are those who appear to be less important, who show themselves in times of crisis where they leave a lasting impression because of acts of decisiveness or heroism. Because of the diverse and fractious nature of life today there is less opportunity for children to assimilate the positive role model qualities found in others. In the modern family there are many challenges to maintain or develop a sense of culture – rules, positive habits, and beliefs which build an environment in which role models can be expressed. Today, technology and the emphases on individual goals and acquisitions do little to build a culture in relationships. It is difficult for a child to form a stable impression of their world when they live in an environment where Warrior traits dominate. There needs to be a strong Chief/Servant synergy present in a child's life for the child to feel a sense of security and order. It is the qualities expressed in family structure and community that form positive role models that give a sense of self and social and of moral values, particularly values that show entitlement is earned.

Scenarios: Following situations show how negative role modelling can carry over to the next generation.

Scenario 1: Money and conflict

> In Thomas's childhood his parents argued constantly over money. Although his father earned a good salary, there was never enough money to pay the bills. Letters threatened action for unpaid bills, and at times the electricity was cut off. The conflict often escalated into fierce arguments and his parents blamed each other.

> Thomas grew up, left home, and married. In turn, Thomas gave his new wife, Emma, what he considered to be sufficient funds in the household budget. When Emma asked for extra money for unexpected expenses, Thomas became frustrated and eventually lost his temper and told her she was not managing their finances properly.

> Before long, the mention of money always started an argument. Jack repeatedly expressed his anger and attacked Emma, and this conflict became central to their relationship. Gradually the anger and resentment caused a rift.

Thomas unconsciously became a powerless child (Infantile Slave) whenever there was conflict over money and then became aggressive (Primitive Chief) in an attempt to gain power over the situation. The situation was a re-enactment of his parents' behaviour.

Scenario 2: Possessions and conflict

> When her mother died, Jean inherited her antique china. As a child, Jean had never been allowed to play with it.
>
> The china was proudly displayed in a cabinet in Jean's house. Her niece often came to visit, bringing her four-year-old daughter, Amy, with her. Jean became highly stressed when Amy visited, as the child wanted to play with the china, and Jean was afraid it might get damaged.
>
> During one visit, Amy took some of the china out of the cabinet and broke a cup. Jean responded by angrily shouting at Amy, who promptly burst into tears.

The inherited territorial relationship to the antiques triggered an automatic response from Jean (Chief), clouding rational thought. Jean's outburst mirrored her mother's response to her antique collection. This shows role modelling can carry from one generation to another.

Who in your life were positive role models?

_____

_____

What qualities did they express that benefit you today?

_____

_____

'Character' surrogates – using others

A surrogate is someone who shares or takes responsibilities on our behalf because we are unable or do not want to take on a particular task. The reasons for our avoiding a task can be numerous, for example time constraints, feeling inadequate, knowing others will do it better or considering it beneath our station. Any one of us may have used another person as a surrogate to support a lack of, or underdevelopment of, a particular 'character' within ourselves. Surrogacy is common in a normal, functioning relationship. This can be seen when parents express a complementary surrogate: one parent may express the organising qualities of the Chief/Servant, and the other may attend to general personal needs expressing the Servant/Chief.
Surrogacy can be positive, as in the case that someone volunteers to stand in for another person. Negative surrogacy can be seen in the use of coercion as a means of manipulating someone to carry out an action that could victimise that person. It could be co-dependency: a person is controlled and manipulated by another using him or her as a substitute to do work that is the manipulative person's responsibility.

An example of a positive surrogacy is where an individual who is a Servant type personality forms a complementary relationship with a Servant/Chief type. This complementary relationship could be enduring, provided each stays in role. In a crisis, however, those roles can change to a negative surrogacy. When the Primitive 'characters' rear their heads a complementary surrogacy is tested, as when one partner exhibits a role that challenges the status quo. For example, a Servant type personality might switch to his or her Warrior, challenging the Chief of the other partner. This situation has two possibilities: a break in the relationship or an accommodation.

Then there is the manipulative use of others as surrogates, such as to encourage someone to carry the risk if things do not work out, when they become a scapegoat. For instance, a manager who either doesn't like an employee or is envious of the employee's success, or both, might encourage a supervisor to make the employee's life difficult, with the aim of getting rid of him or her. The employee would most probably see the supervisor as the perpetrator of their misery. If the issue became a legal matter the manager could deny knowledge of a problem. This would leave the supervisor carrying the responsibility. Another situation is a relationship of convenience, where an individual in a position of power, expressing their Primitive Chief, makes a promise to reward a subordinate who acts on his or her Primitive Warrior to advantage both of them. This type of relationship is often found where there are corrupt or illegal business practices and where people use one another for their own ends.

Another destructive form of the use of a surrogate is when an individual responds from his or her Recalcitrant Slave to seek revenge or gain advantage by setting others up to express their Primitive Warrior. The person acting from the Recalcitrant Slave perspective will target individuals whom he or she knows have existing feelings of discontent, frustration, or of having been done an injustice. These individuals can be incited to behave in a way that avoids the person doing the inciting becoming directly involved (metaphorically, they are putting bullets in the gun, although they are not prepared to shoot it). If others carry out an act of revenge on their behalf they will stand on the sidelines, bearing no responsibility for the consequences.

Further examples of a surrogate are children who call upon their parents' Chief /Servant or Servant/Chief to help them deal with a situation that needs an adult; or employers (Chiefs) hiring staff to act as their Servants, Warriors or Chiefs to help manage their company. Some individuals, to compensate for their underdeveloped 'characters', will form relationships with others. A person who is a Servant type often seeks a relationship with a Chief type and vice versa. Have you ever noticed couples where one seems to have strong Chief qualities while the other has a more Servant personality? This is nature's selective processing to balance the 'character' strengths and weakness of both individuals to form a synergistic relationship.

There are circumstances in which a person is called on to act as a broker to gain peace (Mentor). As you see, surrogates are a necessary ingredient in relationships to work successfully.

Summary of 'character' profiles and their intent

Behaviours to gain status

Maintain status

Primitive Warrior fearful of not acquiring physical and mental needs; emotionally insensitive and callous; will use aggression and intimidation to gain what they want. 'If you get in my way you will reap the consequences!'

Primitive Chief is fearful of loss of status and territory; emotionally insensitive, critical and demanding; will threaten force to maintain order. 'Do as you are told, or you will reap the consequences!'

Warrior/Servant will use every avenue to gain attention for emotional and physical connection; disarms others through social displays of intelligence, physical prowess, sense of fun, and bantering; uses the same techniques to test boundaries. 'I'll have a go at anything! Are you game, or

Chief/Servant will teach and encourage cooperation; shows trust when giving responsibilities to others within the group; considers the physical and emotional capacity of the members; seeks results. 'Do you feel able to take responsibility for this task, or do you need

are you scared?' They could be referred to as the warrior of the tribe.

further information?' They could be referred to as the father of the tribe.

Servant/Warrior has a strong need for reassurance. Relates to others on a personal level through joint interests; works to build feelings of empathy and trust. 'I enjoy your company.' They could be referred to as the adolescent warrior of the tribe.

Servant/Chief has a strong need to relate on a personal level through nurturing, emotional bonding, and physical participation. Encourages others to appreciate their relationships with each other. 'I can see you have a problem. Let me help you.' They could be referred to as the mother of the tribe.

Role conflicts

We may have played roles that did not suit our disposition. This could place stress on us and our relationships. How many of us have had a job or been in circumstances where we have been required to do things that have caused us to behave in a way that is not comfortable? Often this is an indication that your 'character' type is not suited to the situation. Even though you are able to do what is required in practice, emotionally you feel compromised, unable to function optimally. An individual who has been promoted to a manager's role (Chief/Servant) could feel more comfortable with a collegial role (Servant/Warrior). If they feel threatened by the new role, that feeling can cause them to overcompensate and exhibit their Primitive Chief. This will damage their relationships with those they have previously felt connected to.

A shift in status can also cause role confusion, as is found in moving from a formal setting to an informal one. In this situation an individual might have trouble determining which 'character' role she or he should play. For example, if an employee attends a party at the employer's home, the employee may find it difficult to determine if she or he should act from their Servant, waiting to be engaged by the employer, or engage the employer from a Warrior/Servant synergy, showing familiarity. In either approach the role's status is at issue. If you are invited to someone's home you let them set the agenda. This will indicate the roles expected. Provided it is not negative, go with the feeling that makes you comfortable within that situation.

Scenario: Bringing a friend into your business

> John invites his best friend Pat to join his company as a manager. John is keen to work with Pat, as they've been close for years and John has always enjoyed Pat's sense of humour.
>
> At first they work well together; however, John notices that Pat is unable to adjust to being managed and often speaks or behaves inappropriately. His humour is misplaced, and the situation feels awkward.

When Pat is invited to join the company, the relationship between the two friends changed. Pat found it hard to address John as a boss (Chief), John avoided showing leadership in managing his friend in his Servant role. Pat is a Warrior/Servant type in a Servant role. This is a recipe for conflict.

Scenario: Loss of tribal membership

> Jim, office manager for 20 years, is an outgoing person who always seems to be in control. He is unexpectedly made redundant. He withdraws, not only from his family, but from all his usual sporting activities and social commitments.
>
> Occasionally, Jim rewrites his resume and applies for new jobs. With every rejection, however, he becomes increasingly depressed.

The loss of Jim's confidence comes when his Chief/Servant is dismissed. He has been so used to playing that role, he is unable to rely on his other 'characters' to adjust. The lack of flexibility in his 'character' roles does not allow for his readjustment to new circumstances. He has lost his managerial income, his status, and a feeling of purpose. He must find the Warrior in his nature to seek a new job and dig himself out of this situation – real and emotional. Without his Warrior, his Chief will not be able to emerge again.

The unintentional response

Sometimes a situation where we intend to act from a particular 'character' is hijacked by events causing us to act in a way that is totally against our better judgement, doing the exact opposite of what we intended to do. Have you found yourself in any of the following circumstances?

I really wanted to talk things out, to find an agreeable outcome; the conversation started out cordially. The attitude from the other side irritated, causing me to respond in a way that was not intended. A shouting match developed. This was a switch from the Mentor approach to the uncensored Primitive Warrior.

I feel taken for granted and expected to comply with requests. I intended to be assertive and saying 'No!', a Chief/Servant response. But instead I said, 'I would be happy to help!', becoming a Slave.

The internal conflict between our 'characters' will find expression internally or externally, or both. If our Primitive Chief is active, we will harshly criticize others or enslave ourselves through self-criticism and self-condemnation. If our Primitive Warrior is expressed, we will threaten others and we may put ourselves at risk. When we act from our Servant in contributing to the common good and end up feeling like a Slave we have given up our right to be treated fairly. It is important to listen to your internal dialogue and feelings, which will indicate the 'characters'. This can reduce the potential for becoming entangled in emotional mire.

Scenario: Uncensored response

Jenny, the manager of a company, is disappointed and frustrated at the poor attitude and work habits of Paula, an employee. She has spoken to her twice in an effort to sort things out and although she had agreed to be more co-operative, Paula has not changed her behaviour.

Jenny arranges a further meeting in an attempt to resolve the matter. Despite her frustration she decides to approach the issue in a friendly and reasonable way. She considers various ways to help improve the situation and arranges a meeting for 10am the next day. At 10.20am Paula enters her office without knocking, plonks herself down in a chair, and gives Jenny a defiant look. Jenny loses her good intentions and shouts at Paula about her timekeeping, her attitude and all her other inadequacies, and tells her to get out.

Jenny's goal had been to resolve the conflict in a mutually beneficial way (Mentor). However, Paula's flippant attitude (Warrior) overwhelmed Jenny's reasoning, triggering an aggressive response (Primitive Chief)

You may have been in situations where you have felt unjustly treated by others. This may have built up strong feelings of resentment or anger. In such situations, our Primitive 'characters' may express inappropriate dialogue and behaviour. We may lash out. We may even carry out actions to deliberately create problems for a specific person or organisation.

When strong feelings or resentments build up over time, we have a choice as to whether to hold on to them or release them. Repressing or releasing feelings can be habitual. Understanding the internal conflict or dialogue of our 'characters' helps us to make choices consciously.

A healthy release could be obtained from a counsellor or from talking to a trusted friend, from physical exercise, writing a journal or a mixture of all these. This venting of emotions can discharge pent-up energy and allow time for reason to surface. This could help safeguard us from behaving inappropriately or dangerously.

Lies and manipulation

Most of us at some time have told lies. It's part of being human. It is the reason that we lie that is the issue. Even people who think telling lies is wrong will have difficulty avoiding telling them at some time. Lying is giving information with the intent to deceive. It may be used to gain advantage in a situation or with the intention of reducing harm or avoiding conflict. So where do the 'characters' fit into communicating lies? The Chief will lie to maintain power and status, such as using delaying tactics until they can re-enforce their position, whereas the Warrior will lie to put others on the defensive and create opportunity. The Servant uses lies to maintain existing conditions and avoid alienation; they will be prepared to sacrifice the truth in order to maintain a friendship. The Slave lies to avoid pain and persecution. Even the Mentor will tell untruths to prevent the victimisation of or harm to others. Areas where people are prone to untruths are in job interviews, in the spring of a relationship, when faced with being punished, in the business environment and when feeling vulnerable.

Then there are those who use ambiguous or deceptive language to deliberately persuade others to second-guess the actual meaning behind the communication. This is a ploy to leave the communication open to interpretation, which has the potential to produce conflict or victimisation. A tendency to use indirect communication may have originated in early childhood and be carried over into adulthood. This 'not telling the full truth' can be used to protect self or others or to manipulate a situation and could weaken and/or complicate relationships, preventing intimacy. If we have not developed sufficient 'character' synergy, trust and respect for others, boundaries will not be established.

Think of a time you have employed lies that have left you with a question about your intent. For example, your best friend asks your opinion and you lie because to tell the truth may cause your friend to reject you. It is this fear of rejection that sometimes causes us to have conflicts about telling the truth to others. This kind of response comes from the Servant or even Servant/Warrior personality types. Do we tell the truth and be damned or explore the reason for the need for lies or avoidance of the truth? When confronted with this dilemma we have to look at the wider picture, considering how our actions affect others as well as ourselves. Once we identify the 'character' that causes us to feel threatened and the responses it triggers to lie or deceive, we will be better able to mentally and intellectually choose a response with courage in dealing with the fears that are masked by lies.

Web of lies

When a person is influenced by the Primitive Warrior in combination with the Recalcitrant Slave, lies take on a dangerous mix and a web of deception evolves. Individuals influenced by this combination are adept at expressing synergistic behaviours to disguise their intent. They lack true 'character' synergy because they have difficulty feeling empathy, an understanding of things from another's perspective. They use emotions to build rapport with the intention of enslaving others so they will conform to their needs. They do this by applying their intellect in manipulative responses to hide their intentions. They can weave elaborate, fictitious explanations to justify their actions. If caught out, they respond with anger and threats or might construct a new explanation for their actions. They hate to lose any argument or fight and will aggressively defend their web of lies. Their lack of empathy makes them incapable of feeling shame, guilt or remorse. They pursue any action that serves their own self-interest even if it seriously harms others.

These people can be highly adaptive in expressing 'character' synergy, feigning empathetic behaviour. They tend to be highly intelligent, but they use their brain power to deceive others rather than to empower them. This behaviour starts in childhood; they learn how to express synergistic behaviours without developing empathy. Empathy is a feeling of obligation and concern for others. This helps us to restrain our primitive impulses and selfish intent. Empathy can be felt for your own group or for universal humanity. There are varying degrees of empathy, depending on our moods and environment. It is when empathy is absent that there is the danger of deception and manipulation.

Scenarios: power, manipulation and ambiguous Communication

> **1.** An employee tells the manager that there is a problem requiring urgent attention and asks what should be done. The manager, who doesn't want to take responsibility for making a decision, responds, 'Do what you think should be done!'

The manager (Chief), consciously or unconsciously, is using power without responsibility: claiming the benefit if all goes well and disclaiming responsibility if things go wrong. This type of behaviour undermines the confidence of the employee and at the same time asserts and maintains the status of the manager. If the manager acts from his or her Chief/Servant and allows the employee to act on the employee's own initiative, the Chief/Servant would take responsibility for the employee's actions, even if the initiative failed. This type of behaviour would have the effect of building up employee confidence and trust in the Manager.

> **2.** A parent praises a child for completing a task, adding that the job could have been done better if it had been done the way they were told to do it.

The parent (Primitive Chief), by using praise and criticism, is reinforcing her or his own position and at the same time reminding the child of the pecking order. This approach has the effect of controlling the child by making it feel vulnerable (Slave).

3. Jerry's son Mike asks if he can have some beer at his birthday party. Jerry is reluctant to allow this because Mike is still only sixteen. Mike persists, saying, 'Would it be all right if we only have light beers and you and Mum are chaperones for the evening?' Jerry gives in to the request and the party takes place without incident.

A few months later, Jerry opens the refrigerator and is surprised to find a carton of light beer. He speaks to his son about it and Mike admits buying the beer for a friend's party, adding that the friend's parents will be chaperones, just as Jerry was at his own party. Jerry reluctantly accepts the situation.

A few days later Jerry comes home early from work, and finds his son and two of his friends on the settee drinking beer.

Jerry (Servant/Chief) has unknowingly permitted circumstances to develop that weaken his parental control. He gives his son the power to push the boundaries and set his own agenda. Mike (Primitive Warrior) exploits the situation to gain more power by attempting to gradually erode his father's position towards underage drinking.

4. When Pat's husband James dies suddenly, she is left financially and emotionally vulnerable. A neighbour learns of her loss and visits Pat to

offer practical help and support. The visits become more frequent and Pat starts to become dependent on the neighbour's support. Her neighbour-turned-friend begins organising her life more and making decisions on her behalf. Soon Pat feels that she has lost control of her life.

In this type of situation we see a mixture of dynamics where the intent is to be either supportive or exploitative, or a mixture of them both. Intent is not always clearly defined, however, and the underlying motivations might be consciously or unconsciously set out by an individual. Pat's neighbour may have stepped in with good intentions behind his actions, but it is unclear to what degree subtle deceptions might be at play as their role increases and he gains more control over her life.

Ambiguous dialogue masks the 'character' we are expressing in our intentions. The underlying need could be to maintain a relationship, or to take advantage. That is why it is important to be direct with a considered response.

Have you ever been asked by a friend to support them on an issue that goes against your conscience?

If you put aside your own beliefs in order to avoid conflict, you will be faced with your own crisis of values.	If you give your support with the ulterior motive of gaining an advantage in the future, you can damage your own integrity.
If you don't support your friend, you risk being rejected and losing the friendship.	.If you offer to support them and have second thoughts you can be left with a struggle with your sense of loyalty to others.

How aware are you of your own communication style with others? Consider the scenarios you have just read that are similar to ones you have experienced and try to get a clearer view of which 'characters' you played and how they contributed to the way you felt.

Conflict between obligation and how you feel

A person's responses are influenced by complex and sophisticated interactions between the 'characters' within the personality, exhibited in dialogue and gesture. Our responses are not objective but subjective. There are many elements at work e.g., environment, our feelings toward the person we are communicating with, the matter being discussed and our own personal agenda.

We respond to groups or individuals in various ways. The manner will depend on the degree of synergy between our 'characters'. Let's look at a situation where a friend asks you to support a group that is campaigning on a social injustice issue. This example can apply to other situations. You may give one of the following outward responses as found in the left-hand column. The right-hand column shows the internal evaluation of our commitment or its justification.

External Dialogue	Internal Dialogue
Yes I will help but it will be limited.	I don't want this to take up too much of my time. (Warrior/Servant)
What amount of time commitment are you expecting?	How much of my independence am I prepared to surrender? (Warrior/Servant)

I need to give it thought	How much influence will I have in changing things? (Chief/Servant)
If I do this it could be a cost to my reputation.	Am I prepared to fight for the group interest at the expense of my own? (conflict between the Chief/Servant's view and the Primitive Chief).
How long do you expect the protest to take?	What time should I give? (Servant/Warrior)
Is there any other way of gaining justice?	I need to seek options (Servant/Warrior)
I don't want to do anything that is unlawful.	What if things go wrong, how will it affect me? (Servant)
I am not sure if I can be relied on to give a great deal of time.	What am I compromising? (Servant/Warrior)
At what point is the group prepared to accept a compromise?	How does the group reach compromises? (Mentor)

The questions below are all about 'character' synergy, that is, the degree to which our 'characters', working together and influencing each other, help us make better decisions.

You may want to check out your own knowledge by doing the following exercise!

Kerry shares a house with three other people and has become frustrated because the chores previously agreed to be carried out were only being partially completed, or not being done at all. Fed up with constantly completing other peoples' tasks, Kerry decides to take some action and ...

107

Which 'character' or 'characters' are expressed in the following?

1. Demands others take responsibility for carrying out their own chores. (_____)

2. Calls a meeting to discuss the issue. (_____)

3. Blame others for the problem. (_____)

4. Use an encouraging approach to each individual to get him or her to do chores. (_____)

5. Cleans up because he feels no one else will do it. (_____)

6. Decides to clean up his own mess only. (_____)

7. Thinks cleaning is beneath him. (_____)

8. Cleans up because no one else has time to do it. (_____)

9. Quietly finds another place to live. (_____)

10. Avoids doing any tasks. (_____)

11. Verbally attacks others. (_____)

12. Approaches housemates individually, asking them to consider the consequences if the situation continues. (_____)

Answer: 1. Primitive Chief 2. Chief/Servant 3. Slave 4.Servant/Chief 5. Servant/Slave 6. Warrior/Servant 7. Primitive Chief 8. Servant/Chief 9. Servant/Slave 10. Warrior/Servant 11. Primitive Warrior 12 Mentor

Exercise: Find out how you operate in your tribal relationship

This bar graph is an example that illustrates the amount each 'character' expresses in the work and home situation.

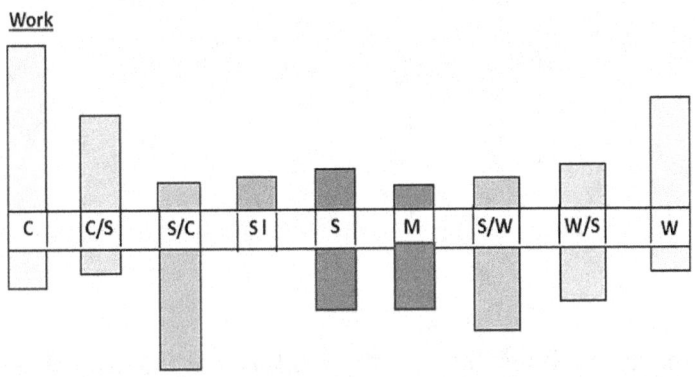

Work

| C | C/S | S/C | S I | S | M | S/W | W/S | W |

Home

This particular graph shows an individual in the work situation is overbearing and controlling work. At home they are more amenable. The bar graph illustrates an individual's behaviour can be different at home than in the work situation.

Character' abbreviation: C-Chief, CS-Chief/Servant, SC-Servant/Chief, Sl-Slave, S-Servant, M-Mentor, SW-Servant/Warrior, WS-Warrior/Servant, W-Warrior.

Below are two exercises. The first is designed to give a general indication of your tribal disposition in a work and home situation. The other exercise is to show compatibility. Shade in the 'character' column that indicates the 'characters' that are expressed strongly in your personality in these two situations using a 1 to 5 scale: 1 = Never, 2 = Seldom. 3 = Sometimes, 4 = Often, 5 = Most of the time. For example, if your 'character' is Servant most of the time fill in the full column.

Your 'character' types in the work and home situations

Work

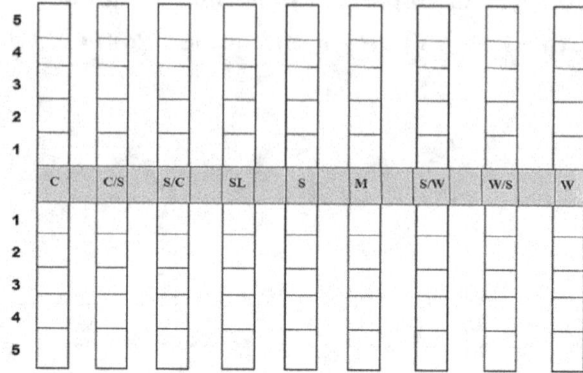

Home

What have you found out from the Work/Home Tribal-gram about yourself? _____

_____

This graph looks at compatibility; person A) has greater flexibility and a strong Servant and Mentor in their personality; this may allow them to influence the strong Warrior and Chief in person B) in a positive way. Another example of plotting your relationship compatibility:

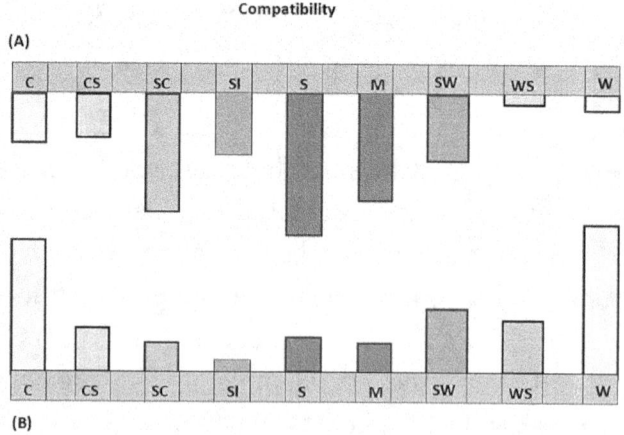

Compatibility Tribal-gram

Person A.

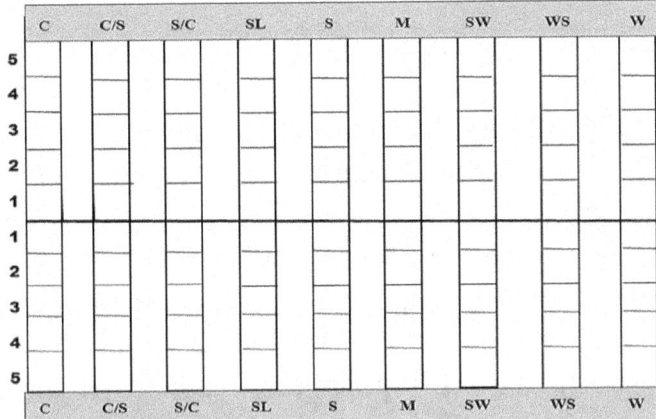

Person B.

What have you found out from the compatibility Tribal-gram about yourself and the other individual?

_____

_____

_____

_____

_____

Part Three: Tribal membership, conflict and challenge

Tribal hierarchy and our needs

All biological systems have some form of hierarchy of needs to sustain them in their environment. The hierarchy of needs specifies behaviours the organism has to acquire to meet these needs. So in this Part we examine the attributes of behaviours that deliver the different requirements to sustain humans in a state of equilibrium. In human beings the 'characters' have particular traits that are specialised in prioritising the needs required for survival.

The diagram below is adapted from Abraham Maslow's hierarchy of needs. Maslow was a leading humanistic psychologist who promoted the notion of self-actualization. We have adapted his model because it helps illustrate the basic human motivations in the tribal connection. We show how the needs of each 'character' contribute to specific qualities in tribal development and how this creates a hierarchy of needs. In ascending order, the pyramid has biological and physical needs, exhibited by the Primitive 'characters'; the emotional needs, show in the Servant. Then there are the physical and emotional social needs found in the 'characters' in synergy that produce our tribal nature. The Mentor represents a state of awareness of self, understanding the action and intent of the other 'characters and incorporates their attributes to humanistic goals.

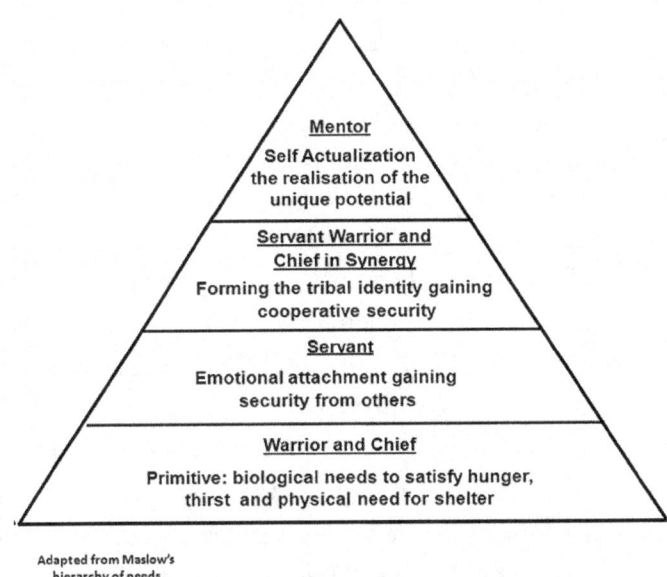

Adapted from Maslow's
hierarchy of needs

For the **Primitive Warrior**, needs are biological: they are to satisfy hunger and thirst and to gain comfort by exploiting the environment. The reasoning is based on acquisitiveness.

For the Primitive **Chief**, needs are physical: they are to control, to define and to defend territory. Reasoning is based on ownership.

The failure to meet Primitive needs can be a source of stress, aggression and physical conflict. Primitive 'characters' act from feelings of being threatened.

For the **Servant** needs are physical and also encompass emotional security. Reasoning is based on the rendering of services and loyalty, with the intent to create emotional attachments and to oblige others to look after the Servant's needs.

The **Servant, Warrior and Chief synergy** forms the tribal nature in which there is a need to maintain identity with others. This synergistic relationship brings together the qualities of each 'character' for the benefit of the individual in relationship to the group, which can involve psychological, social, sexual, personal, cultural, political, or religious factors. Reasoning is based on building co-operation that will benefit the group.

The **Mentor** is a condition of self-actualisation, having the ability to form ethical positions that are fully internalised and independent of the other 'characters'. This allows the recognition of oneself, others, events and situations in real time. It confers the ability to assess objectively the impact of actions on situations and others, and to be introspective in learning from experience. Reasoning is based on the standpoint of doing no harm – evaluating experiences in a non-prejudicial way. If you are acting from one of the other characters you are never aware of your true self. It is in the Mentor that we achieve a state of self.

As you will see, each 'character' has a distinct responsibility regarding survival. It is important for the long-term stability of a relationship that the qualities of 'characters' synergy and of the Mentor are involved. The 'characters' that function in synergy act as counters to each other, stabilising the relationship. This develops and maintains co-operation, which allows for accommodation and restraint of personal differences, bringing together all the qualities of the 'characters' in synergy. This stabilises relationships and helps to form tribal identity. This balance changes when one of the primary 'characters', Warrior, Chief or Servant, becomes dominant in a relationship. Such dominance has a detrimental effect on the stability of that relationship, on either a tribal or personal level. The main reason needs are not met is because one 'character' has sway over the others, causing dissatisfaction and alienation on a personal level, at a tribal level a threat to cohesion.

For people to feel that each level of their needs e.g. safety, food, and physical and emotional connection is being satisfied requires the development of a management system that gives stable governance. The tribal management system developed to manage wars (maintain safety), prepare for famine (manage food supply) and maintain tribal identity (build physical and emotional dependency). The hierarchy of needs diagram shows the steps in our development in meeting these needs. It is in the 'characters' synergy' (tribal state) that we are most likely to have most of our needs satisfied.

The kind of environment for these needs to be met is a tribal society where change is slow and there is strong character synergy in culture and traditions, which bind people together. This encourages people to establish their identity with others through co-operating and working to maintain group rituals and customs. Most rituals and customs were built on celebrating the victories of war, bringing in a good harvest and on common values found in religions that brought emotional benefit and comfort in people's relationship with each other.

In the rapidly changing society we see today they is a fragmenting of the sense of identity and obligation to our group. Individualism is seen as the most important value today. The sense of belonging to a culture is replaced by individualism – the need to satisfy self by acquiring material possessions and social status. This is a step down the needs table to our Primitive needs that are devoid of emotional connection to people but to things. The question is whether we have really become advanced societies.

The search for the meaning and purpose of life usually comes directly from the desire to attain a stable identity, that is, one that comes from a realistic perception of self and from being affirmed by others. People need some form of stability in life to feel they have a purpose and are valued. Meeting tribal needs is essential: without that, life becomes a fight for survival.

115

How our tribal hierarchical management structures fashion culture

The tribal management system's function is to manage change while still maintaining cohesion between the 'character' roles individuals play. The system is successful when personal interest and group interests are in balance. This is shown by people acting out the different roles while seeming to have a different status and different likes and dislikes but still having the same group interests. A culture that has flexibility in acknowledging differences in beliefs, values and norms an individual has within their group indicates a balanced 'character synergy'. Another important need is that a tribe has a central philosophy or belief that characterises people's personal and group interests.

When tribes formed, an organisational structure evolved. It grew out of the need to manage the acquisition of food and shelter and the building of relationships. This organisational template is embedded in all human activities. It is shaped by the 'characters', each of which symbolises an individual's role and also indicates their rank. This established the individual's role and importance in the management process and its cultural protocols. When a person is given a role, in contributing to the regulation of tribal activities they are expected to express the 'character' attributes of that role.

The bringing together of the 'characters' in synergy made the tribal management system successful. The specialised roles provided, when coordinated, an effective way of dealing with the environment. It was these abilities that gave individuals and groups inventive approaches in dealing with changing situations. The impact of the 'characters' people played and their environment, plus the development of tools, advanced cognitive thinking and problem solving. These elements are always in a

116

state of flux, producing the diversity in cultures we see today. It is still important to note that the way in which individuals or groups manage 'character' roles will determine how successful they are in managing their society. Because life is always open to challenges from unexpected events, change is inevitable. A strong synergy between the 'characters' people play within tribal management is important to counter the adverse effects of change. There are however unfortunate situations where a tribe is threatened and its members turn to an individual who they think has the capacity to protect their interests. Often these individuals have a Primitive Warrior profile. They have their own agenda that is shrouded. Their promises enable them to gain power by offering reassurance while accruing power. When in a position of power, these individuals will show their Primitive Chief by coercion and the use of the tribal management system and its institutions to retain their prize, forcing the capitulation of tribal members to their will: or, in other words, dictatorship.

The hierarchical management structure maintains the civil and social values of a tribe. It is the varying character types that fashion the type of culture we have. Historically, there was less freedom than we see today. The 'character' synergy within groups was not as strong, though the structure did to some degree restrain the Primitives by the roles being defined to a specific status that reflected a social class. Today we do not refer to people as being in a social class. People today are able to evaluate their own position in society. Each role is important in an organisational context. However, we do give specific roles a higher social status, such as those that have direct power. The Chief uses direct power to organise through goal setting, planning and delegating, which maintains the tribe's political culture and its management. The Servant plays a supporting role, administering and maintaining communication between the

117

different areas within the tribe to maintain cohesion. The Servant is also involved in production, utilising the tribe's assets to maximise survival and profitability. Warriors provide the connection between the tribe and the wider environment, which includes other tribes. The Warrior acquires assets to allow the organisation to grow. These functions of controlling, asset gaining and serving are found in all societies. Slave status is not always appreciated because it does not have a direct influence on tribal management. The Slave's tasks are often menial, for example, maintaining utilities. It is how strong or weak the synergy is between the character roles and the environment's impact on these roles that determines the type of culture that will evolve.

The tribal management system holds together all the elements that we find in a culture. Culture is symbolic communication constituting the distinctive nature of a tribe's experience and creativity. A culture is a complex system: an individual's role is not stark black and white. It evolves from the way the synergistic strengths and weaknesses between the 'characters' within a tribe is established. There is a range of behaviours that are reflected in the 'characters'' synergies. For example, if the Warrior/Servant types have a strong influence on the tribe the culture would have a hedonistic emphases; a doctrine that pleasure or happiness is the sole goal in life. Whereas the Servant/Warrior is driven by social issues, the concern for the welfare of the dis-advantaged. Servant/Warriors would seek to change the culture from within. The Chief/Servant types would influence the managing of the culture by balancing individuals' needs for interdependence with their independence needs. To put this into a social context conservative values oppose liberal values. Servant/Chief types have more of a supervisory function; to protect the cultural norms and values with a one-on-one approach to managing the cultural principles. If the Primitive Chief is strong, an autocratic rule will prevail; if the Primitive Warrior dominates, the prevailing atmosphere would be openly divisive.

Elements that fashion tribal culture

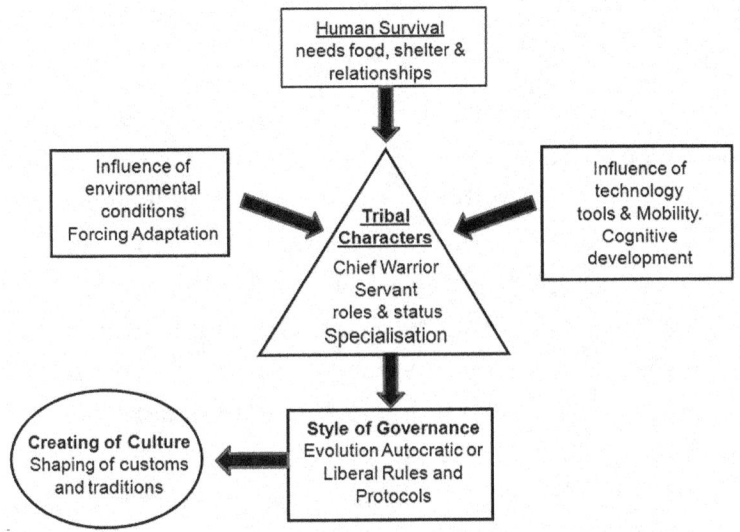

Our need for survival has to be met; a coordinated approach has to be devised allocating specialised roles to meet these needs. Next is to counter the negative influences of the environment by developing skills and tools that improve the ability to counter environmental change. If the environment's effects are positive, then a more liberal approach to managing the tribe will possibly form. If the environment is harsh then a more authoritarian managing of the tribe is likely to develop. Cultural variation comes from the impact of all these forces on individuals and the tribe as a whole.

To explain how tribal structures form and the situations that affect the way they are organised, we use a castaway theme. If we were to place a group of 20 individuals on an island to see how they survived, we would see the 'characters' develop. First, the group would have to assess each other's skills and how they could be applied to provide food and shelter. As priorities are identified, roles and status would develop while the group searched for solutions to their survival needs. Individuals would start expressing the 'character' roles that best suit their personality and skills.

Often an individual who is believed to have strong Warrior skills and enough influence will assume the role of Chief. Such a person would be identified as being able to build alliances and as having the skill to organise and delegate. Once the Chief's position is established the other Warrior types will take the initiative in gaining resources and developing tools and weapons. The Servant types would willingly offer to prepare food, carry goods and help in general. Some individuals might take on more than one role. If resources are found to be insufficient to satisfy the demands of the group divisions will often develop, led by people wanting to be leaders. This could bring about subterfuge and violence. A strong Warrior might emerge demanding obedience as a way of demonstrating leadership. Often in these situations if the Warrior type gains power he or she will move to their Primitive Chief. Alternatively a Mentor could emerge, encouraging peaceful negotiations. The needs of a developing society require individuals to undertake specific roles. Once the group has established a management structure, then codes of behaviour will evolve naturally and a civil society may come into being, forming a culture.

If a tribe's culture is strongly influenced by the Chief the culture will be more hierarchical and conformist to maintain the norms and values of the tribe, whereas if it is influenced by the Warrior there would be a more non-conformist, liberal approach in the culture's development. Today we see this in the conservative versus the liberal view in the political arena and in society in general. The positions between the Warrior and Chief have the potential to cause conflict. The Servant or Mentor brings civility through accommodation.

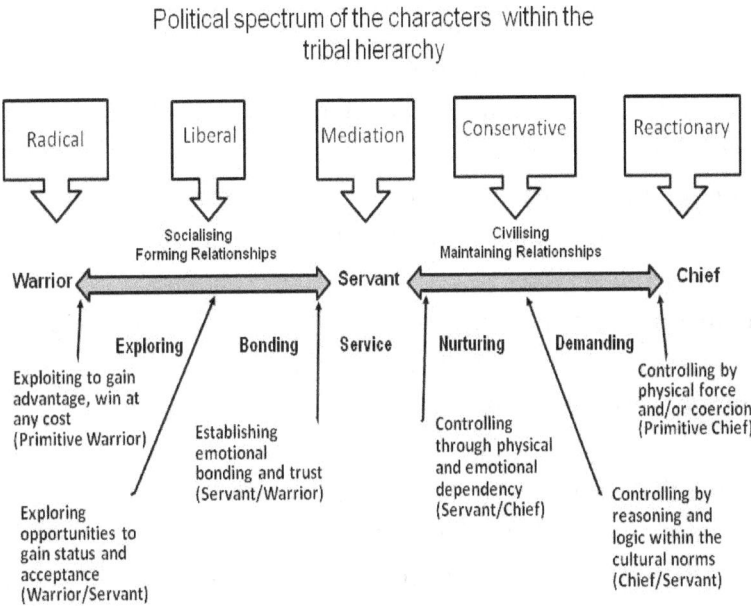

Throughout history there has always been tension between the Chief – the ruling class – and the Warrior – the enterprise class. Unfortunately, the Servant and Slave classes become the victims of any conflict between these two forces. When synergy forms between the 'characters' within an individual, alliances are more likely to emerge that will produce an overall better result than if each person works toward his or her own goals. As we have mentioned, synergy is where the different traits of 'characters' combine to produce a greater adaptive capacity that improves the chances of the survival of the individual and the group.

Socialising and civilising within relationships

The influence of 'characters' on our perceptions and motivations

A relationship has two parts: socialising the development of relationships is the *informal* part and civilising the consolidation is the *formal* of a relationship. It starts with our upbringing, which influences the development of our 'characters' and therefore of the types of relationships we form throughout life. Positive life experiences may restrain the propensity to express Primitive behaviour by bringing the Primitive Chief and Primitive Warrior into synergy with the Servant's feelings of obligation and service. If, because of life experiences, we become empathetic in our nature, we strengthen the synergy between our 'characters'. Empathy acts as a filter against instinctive or primitive responses. We now consider others before taking action. The Mentor may evolve from these processes, giving a person the ability to be objective by identifying and understanding our 'characters' and the prejudices and motives behind them. When experiencing the feelings of powerlessness of the Slave state, we can learn to engage the Mentor to evaluate the circumstances and the way we feel about them, using our ability to assess and control our emotions.

When we socialise, it can be the start of the building of friendships and the formation of partnerships. It can also be a time of testing and challenging the emotional, mental and physical boundaries of others to gain confidence to move towards understanding or intimacy. An initial understanding does not guarantee success in relationships. It is the flexibility of the 'characters' within the synergy that determines success or failure. The 'characters' play a central role in the formation and maintenance of relationships.

A new relationship almost always engenders powerful emotions, from physical curiosity and a desire to explore and express feeling with openness to possibilities. In the early stages, there are few rules and an informal 'social' approach may be used to test the potential of the relationship. Once a degree of trust and status has been established, the relationship may move to the stage of forming rules of engagement, which may result in commitment. If commitment is established, the rhythms and patterns of behaviour can become customary, creating a more formal 'civil' approach adhering to the norms created in the relationship. It may then become a relationship with benefits, as well as degrees of limitations on freedom.

In any relationship there is some degree of weighing up the benefits and the loss of freedom. A socialised and civilised relationship allows for some flexibility in meeting the needs of individuals. The same applies in group relationships. The 'characters' in synergy form socializing and civilizing behaviours, enable a meaningful relationship to develop. Becoming socialised, we express a congenial approach to the needs of others, whether individuals or a group. When we become civilized we accept moral boundaries and express socially acceptable behaviour. It is the tribe that civilises the primitive mind by encouraging one's ability to identify with an individual or one's group, leading to the process of tribalisation; to identify strongly with others and to be loyal to individuals or groups.

The following diagram shows the transition the Primitive Characters make when forming a closer emotional bond with the Servant, producing a socialised and civilised relationship.

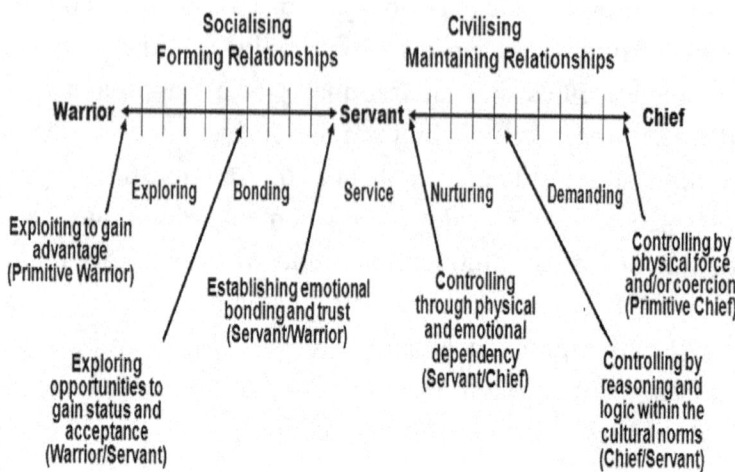

The first stage of forming a relationship is the **socialisation phase**, in which the Warrior/Servant and Servant/Warrior are engaged in testing for compatibility traits. When the Warrior/Servant engages in forming a relationship, the approach will involve light-hearted and playful behaviour to gain acceptance and to explore common interest. This reduces tension and gives a sense of assurance. There is also a search for pleasure in the dynamics. When the Servant/Warrior is engaged, the approach is to build trust and commitment to form intimacy and potential for continuity.

The second stage of a relationship is the **civilising phase**, in which the Chief/Servant and Servant/Chief are engaged in establishing the culture of the relationship. The formal approach involves the Chief/Servant, who implements activities such as task allocation and coordination in achieving a consolidation of the relationship. The Servant/Chief tends to be highly verbal and participatory and expresses a less formal approach in building emotional connection and rapport to maintain intimacy.

Once we are in a relationship, the Warrior in synergy gives it renewal and variety, while the Chief maintains uniformity and social organisation. If we achieve one without the other, the relationship will suffer. A constant striving for uniformity negates renewal and variety. A relationship needs the appropriate flexibility between the 'characters' to sustain it. If a partner often wants to party (Warrior/Servant) or if life is always being structured to a schedule (Chief/Servant) this will diminish commitment over time and resentments will build. This resentment can find an outlet in the Recalcitrant Slave or Primitive Warrior.

Relationship chemistry

In the chemistry of a relationship people will approach a problem in different ways, which can show their qualities and how they can or cannot work with other people. Let's look at a situation where two people enjoy bush walking, but one may have greater confidence. That individual – a Warrior/Servant type – might not want extensive planning and might even enjoy unexpected challenges. The other person is a Servant/Chief type and might want a lot of practical planning before setting out. The two 'characters' might find a way to work together; if they do, that is due to a shift in their 'characters' to a more empathetic position, appreciating the other's contributions, and finding a way to meet the needs of both. Planning for contingencies can be used as a backup if they meet difficulties in their activities, while still leaving the main option as adventure.

The early stages of a relationship are often influenced by the Warrior and Servant in synergy. When a relationship develops further, individuals can feel free to show and explore more of the potential of the relationship. Once a routine and rhythm forms, the Servant/Chief in synergy will emerge; a 'culture' starts to

125

develop, defining the way in which the relationship grows and how it is maintained.

Forming a relationship can be fraught with challenges. In the early discovery stages circumstances dictate the way individuals reveal or omit information about their history. Revealing or omitting often relates to how comfortable a person is in the relationship. There is a learning period, a time of adjustment, at the beginning of relationships. There may be some compatibility, but often there is a time of learning about a person's dominant 'character' type. This is important in strengthening compatibility: without there might be insufficient to continue.

In the past, social norms and institutions played a large part in the way people behaved in forming and maintaining relationships. There was an expectation that you lived with the good and the bad in the relationship and sought to find compromise. This applied particularly to women. This is not to argue that this approach is ideal, only that it tended to bind people to each other.

Over the past 70 years social changes have left few foundations on which people can build an enduring relationship. In the light of these changes, the roles people play are very diverse. Individuals do not want to be tied to one role and resent any expectation that would limit their freedom of choice. What we see is a fracturing of relationships. The only thing people have to rely on is personal promises, which are often not reliable. This type of environment is not conducive for a culture of trust or the achievement of a consistent 'character' synergy in a relationship. Because of the changes in society today we are rapidly losing the character synergy in our tribal relationships. Those relationships create a culture that has customs and rituals that are reliable references, indicating a benchmark of acceptable behaviour, and that give individuals a way of conducting their relationships. There is a problem with this statement: we all want some degree of freedom. That is where the discussion starts: what is an appropriate amount of freedom and what is an appropriate degree of the values that are needed to build and maintain trust. A relationship has to have 'characters' in synergy to gain the best outcome for both parties. That also applies to groups. The Mentor or Chief/Servant are suitable 'characters' to manage conflict issues encountered in relationships.

When people form relationships the initial emotional dynamics can hide underlying past issues that can impact on the future. These issues may have a major influence on the person you choose as a partner or the people you choose as friends. To understand these influences you have to consider your 'characters': do they complement or conflict with those of others. For instance, if you are predominantly a Warrior/Servant type and the other person is a Chief/Servant, you would have a relationship involving high drama, because the other person would expect a somewhat formal approach to the way things are done, whereas you would want a relaxed approach. As another example, if you were a Chief/Servant type in a relationship with a Servant/Chief, it would be a reasonably comfortable but not very exciting relationship; it would lack the input of the Warrior, which adds spice to the relationship.

Individuals who are Warrior/Servant types need to be coaxed into shifting to the Servant/Warrior for a relationship to deepen. When you look at the 'characters' in their synergistic combinations you will see what qualities are best suited for the many issues that a particular relationship faces. It is important, however, to be as flexible as possible in an attempt to find mutual understanding about the roles each plays. If an individual has a tendency to express the qualities that are predominant in their

127

personality, it will cause stress in the relationship in the long term.

Other issues play a part in the ways choices are made and they can have a profound effect on a person's judgement. When individuals form relationships in times life-changing circumstances occur, those events frequently dictate the way in which people respond, which may not be true to their nature. They may express 'characters' that do not reflect their dominant 'characters', those which they would express in more stable conditions. Those they engaged with at that time might have the wrong perception of their true 'character' type. For example, a person after a relationship breakup feels emotionally overwhelmed. They feel like an Infantile Slave. Before the breakup they were in command of their life. Their vulnerability may cause them to engage in a relationship with someone whose character type is not suited to theirs. This could have detrimental effect later in the relationship.

Even in the best of circumstances, individuals can make poor judgments as to the qualities of the person they are forging a relationship with. The reason is often that there is guardedness about how much information should be revealed. This can create problems later, where honesty would have given those involved the opportunity to make an informed choice.
Each of the 'characters' an individual can express has a unique quality. Each 'character' has both positive and negative qualities, and the interplay of these qualities can create variety and drama. The way in which these qualities are managed will depend on self-understanding, the degree of which a person possesses is shown in how the 'characters' are expressed.

Following are situations in which an individuals' true 'character makeup' is often unclearly represented, because of the uncertain position they find themselves in, e.g. subject to emotional confusion and possible deceptions.

1. **Early euphoria**

   There are situations in which, when individuals start to form relationships, their anxieties may be suppressed by strong mental, emotional and physical attraction. Infatuation can often obscure the make-up of their 'characters'. The 'characters' they express at that time may not be consistent with their normal behaviour.

2. **Crisis recovery**

   If an individual forms a relationship with a person who is going through, or just emerging from, a difficult relationship, the nature of their 'characters' may be strengthened or weakened by the experience. When the crisis has passed they may discover the 'character' dynamics between them are not complementary, bringing conflict to the new relationship. Illness, mental or physical elements are factors in obscuring the true nature of a 'character nature and can cause an individual to choose partners who are not compatible.

3. **Intentional omission**

   In an early relationship, an individual may defer (temporarily or indefinitely) the disclosure of information, hiding truths about themselves that they fear might prejudice the relationship. Presenting themselves in the most acceptable way by hiding something may spring from our Servant's fear of a negative response, or from our Warrior attempting to gain advantage. Either way, this is a protective action in the early phase of a relationship.

There is no specific combination of 'characters' that achieves a 'perfect' balance. Relationships are organic, with the capacity for change. People can choose to reconfigure their relationship by making decisions beneficial to both parties. With effective communication and sufficient compromise – *and with a clear understanding of the way 'characters' work in the relationship* – fresh beginnings or amicable endings are possible.

Hazards in forming relationships

The unstructured nature of forming a relationship leaves us vulnerable to making wrong decisions. The true nature of an individual's personality can be masked in the early stages. That is why judgments can be clouded and decisions made can have future ramifications that were not envisaged. If we know the type of our 'characters' type and those of our partner then we will be less vulnerable after the 'honeymoon' phase of the relationship. Problems can occur if there is a strong Chief or Warrior characters dominant in the relationship. An awareness of the way we make our choices can assist us to make better-considered judgments and help us to avoid relationships with the potential to become divisive and abusive.

Have you had the experience of engaging in a relationship with someone who has traits similar to those of a person from your past? This may be because we are naturally predisposed toward patterns of continuity. As we build relationships we may re-create similar patterns that we see or observe from our own past. This can make it difficult to determine what type of relationship we are getting ourselves into. We may accept behaviour that goes against our true nature. This can create internal conflict, making it difficult to establish a sense of emotional stability. Already learnt behaviours can easily affect our judgment when forming relationships. We may have developed a Slave disposition formed from relationship conditioning, experienced in childhood, causing us to put up with an uncomfortable relationship similar to the ones we have experienced or observed. On the other hand we may have a strong Chief expressing our needs to dominate or to feel in control, or a Warrior expressing our need to vent frustrations. In either of these approaches, understanding our 'characters' and their interactions will help us see clearly what kind of relationships we are forming or have formed.

Ability to form and maintain personal relationships

Our 'character' types can change subtly or dramatically. This will depend on the 'character' type of the individuals with whom we form relationships. Some changes will be obvious, others not so. Initially we might be unaware of them, until a situation amplifies them. This can be found where a person gradually switches 'character' type, for example from Servant/Chief, taking responsibility for looking after the household and the personal interests of our partner to beginning to express a Warrior/Servant 'character' more strongly, going out on social outings regardless of what is needed at home. The other partner often consciously or subconsciously knows there is a change in the relationship. They can feel confused and unable to identify what has changed. Often the underlying feelings will be shown in dissatisfaction, and can be intensified in crises.

The interchange within roles is often seamless in a well-functioning relationship, when each person accedes to the change of roles. If one partner expresses their Warrior/Servant, suggesting they sort out a movie and invite the neighbours over for drinks to cap off the day, the other might express their Servant/Chief, saying they will put a few snacks together, after they get the children off to bed. Or consider a different example, involving a stressful situation. One partner expresses their

131

Primitive Chief, showing annoyance at the children's non-cooperation at bedtime. He or she shouts at the children, demanding they do as they are told. The other partner gives support by showing a united front, but feels the need to discuss a different approach to managing the issue. In stressful situations we are prone to expressing 'characters' that are not appropriate, particularly the Primitives. When we strengthen our recognition of the 'characters' we can recover our responses more quickly.

Here are some of the qualities of 'characters' that have a beneficial influence on a relationship. If a partnership is based on Chief/Servant synergy dialogue will be reasoned and logical, focusing on finding a satisfactory outcome that protects each person's integrity. While in previous centuries males have been central to decision making in the marriage, having unquestioned power (Primitive Chief) over their partner (Servant or Slave), today the Chief/Servant synergy is equally important to both men and women; and so is the Mentor. This complicates the relationship of course, as it calls for greater flexibility in the way people express their roles.

Relationships have two parts: rejuvenation and maintenance. Rejuvenation involves the Warrior/Servant and Servant/Warrior in keeping the relationship fresh. Maintenance is where the Chief/Servant and Servant/Chief are important in keeping the general culture of the relationship intact. Understanding the roles is important, and so is flexibility in making a relationship work. When each partner can accommodate the other's varying 'character' dispositions in a changing environment, with input from the Mentor, strengthening intimacy can be achieved. People who have difficulty in being flexible in their use of 'character' roles will perpetuate an unhealthy relationship, which may go on for years or end in an abrupt departure. The stored-up resentment may find its expression in the Recalcitrant Slave, open conflict or physical and mental illness.

Scenarios: Different approaches to maintaining tribal relationships

1. Two parents are discussing how to deal with the attitude of a child who has been breaking the rules. One parent suggests extra chores be given as a way of teaching obligation (Chief/Servant). The other parent suggests the child be given a warning and told that the issue will be treated more seriously next time (Servant/Chief).

A parent who feels unable to cope with their child gives up and withdraws into depression (Servant/Slave). If, however, he or she becomes angry, severe punishment may be threatened: 'If you do that again...!' The parent might kick the kid out of the house, or inflict physical punishment (Chief).

2. Joanne and Jeff's home life has become stressful. They both work full time, which results in the neglect of general housekeeping, which causes tension. Tasks are carried out haphazardly or not at all, and each of them thinks the other isn't pulling their weight.

Joanne gets upset at what is going on and decides to plan a routine of 'Rules to live by' in order to resolve the problem. Jeff is reluctant to respond positively to a program foisted upon him, until they discuss the plan and its benefits together, at which point Jeff even makes helpful suggestions.

This scenario demonstrates the shifting roles in a relationship, from both feeling like Slaves; neither has taken responsibility for the mess around the home, which is causing tension. Joanne's way of dealing with it is to express her Chief/Servant and draw up some rules, whereas Jeff initially responds from his Recalcitrant Slave. When discussions take place he switches to Servant/Chief, then together they work toward an arrangement that suits both of them.

> **3.** Jack does not complete a job on time and is severely reprimanded by his employer and ordered to complete the job immediately. Jack breaks down and confesses he couldn't cope with what he had been asked to do on his own. His employer then changes his attitude and suggests that someone could help Jack get the job completed. Jack, however, is still distressed and his employer suggests he take time off to recover.

This scenario demonstrates several different roles of Jack's employer: Chief ('you'll do what you're told') to Chief/Servant ('we'll get you help so you can finish the task') to Servant/Chief ('let's take care of you').

Change in status and its effect on relationships

A change in the status of individuals can have a profound effect on them and their relationships. This alteration to status forces them to change the roles they have previously played. They have to adjust their internal 'characters' to respond or behave accordingly – this is not always easy when roles have become part of our culture (patterned behaviour). When this occurs we have become emotionally attached to the roles we play, which makes it difficult to take in the reality of our situation. In other words, personality change is being forced on us by circumstances. Consequently, the individuals may experience depression, anxiety, alienation, confusion or even envy. Perceptions of power and expectations (of self and others) can also change in such circumstances. Conversely, if a person has flexibility in 'character' synergy she or he is more inclined in a positive way by the changes and happy with new experiences.

Some examples of situations that reflect changes in status:

- personal tragedy - major accident, death of a friend or family a member
- job or financial loss
- inheriting or winning a considerable amount of money
- unexpected immoral or unethical behaviour in someone we esteemed
- promotion or demotion
- retirement
- reduction in authority
- reduction in responsibility
- divorce
- preferential treatment (of employee, family member, schoolkid, etc)
- relocation
- loss of contact with specific people
- change in working conditions
- Relationship change – sibling gets married, parents' divorce, best friend gets married, having a child etc.

Any of these things could happen to us, and indeed, some of them probably already have. Our ability to manage situations depends on the flexibility we are able to exercise in using our 'characters'. A marked shift in 'characters' will always have an effect on our relationships and will inevitably occur when confronted with a change in status.

Scenario: An unexpected change of status

> Benny has been responsible for setting up and running the company computer system for sixteen years. He is proud of the consistent quality of the systems and his diligent upgrades.
>
> When the company merges with another, the new management brings in its own consultants to handle the integration of the computer systems. When Benny hears second-hand about the ongoing discussions he is furious at not being asked to be involved and at the lack of recognition of his status and expertise.
>
> When the consultants eventually approach Benny for technical information to enable them to import data from his system on to the new system, Benny refuses to disclose all the relevant and necessary technical information and even introduces a virus into the system.

Benny's loss of status, coupled with the company's disregard for his skills and long-term contribution, bring out his Recalcitrant Slave. When the resentment builds sufficiently, he acts in a vengeful manner (Warrior).

Emotional obstacle to communication

Often strong feelings in a conflict can be a negative conduit for past hurtful experiences, intensifying emotions in the present. The emotions can flood the senses and block the formation of 'character' synergy and, also, access to the Mentor, thus making it unlikely a person can use his or her emotional intelligence to effect change by identifying and assessing the 'characters' involved and so control his or her emotions.

The use of reasoning does not itself suggest a problem is understood clearly or that the proper action will follow. But by identifying the 'characters' involved and assessing intention we have greater understanding of why we feel as we do. We can then apply 'characters' that will help us gain control over our emotions. Reasoning is a deductive process that that gives us a mental structure to help us reach some form of decision or action. A person can be taught to engage the logical and reasoning 'characters' to override an emotional morass. They can contrast the emotional descriptions of the feeling with reasoning to construct a response that deals with feelings in a constructive manner.

If we are strongly influenced by emotions we may vent them through our Primitives or suppress them through the Slaves. We are vulnerable to conflict, which will often be detrimental to a positive result in case of disputes. We could follow a destructive path – powerlessness (Infantile Slave), then feelings of resentment or revenge (Recalcitrant Slave), and finally, violent action (Primitive Warrior). If we express this type of temperament we will often be a prisoner of our own emotions.

When we are subject to circumstances that cause us to feel powerless, engaging the Servant/Warrior to explore cautiously where change is needed can offer a way forward. Then we can engage the Chief/Servant to become informed and organised, building our confidence to make changes. Finally, we can engage the Warrior/Servant to act on this information. These 'characters' in synergy help us make sure change does not jeopardize our security.

The synergistic combinations help us to evaluate options by considering actions strategically while protecting our dignity, strengthening our sense of self and being conscious of others in the relationship.

The following scenarios illustrate some negative emotional behaviour that will often have long-term ramifications, such as exploitation, loss of self-control and insensitivity, which can be damaging in a major way.

Scenario: Uncensored behaviour

> Kent often abused Betty, his partner of many years. Betty's friend tells her she shouldn't allow him to treat her in this way. Betty listens to her friend but feels powerless.
>
> One day, when Kent comes home and starts to shout at her, Betty's anger and frustration boil over. She attacks him in the most furious way, causing him to flee the house.

Betty has endured years of abuse and her fear has dominated. She is somewhat buoyed emotionally by the support of her friend (who expressed the Warrior/Servant, suggesting she confront Kent, instead of suggesting getting outside support, which would have been a better option), but she still does not feel strong enough to act against the abuse (Infantile Slave). On the day she attacked Kent she was totally unaware of the Primitive Warrior that had been unleashed. She acted on feelings that had smouldered for years. She was not in control of her emotions as her Primitive Warrior asserted itself.

Scenario: Payoff

Carol has just recently split from Darren. Bill, a friend of both Carol and Darren, comes round to commiserate and offer support. He recognizes Carol's vulnerability and sees the opportunity for himself.

In this type of situation, individuals are open to exploitation. If Carol accepts Bill's attention, she may become a victim of deception: 'I can't tell him I am not interested because he was so good to me when I was in need.' The reverse of this could be that Carol accepts all the help and attention she can get, and when Bill's services are no longer required, she can say: 'Goodbye!'

The relationships in this scenario demonstrate how boundaries may be tested and dependencies built (Warrior), and how, when the deception is successful, a controlling attitude (Chief), may emerge.

Scenario: Betrayal

When her late mother's last will and testament is read, Jenny begins to cry. She is upset when she hears that the diamond engagement ring promised to her has been left to one of the grandchildren. Her sister Penny suggests she should grow up and accept the situation. Her brother Peter says they should honour their mother's wishes. Her brother Patrick puts his arm around her and tries to comfort her.

Hurt and upset at the broken promise, Jenny feels rejected and vulnerable (Infantile Slave). Her sister's indifferent response (Chief) compounds her feelings of alienation. Peter wants the matter to be conducted in a civilised and honourable way (Chief/Servant). The third sibling, Patrick, offers support (Servant/Chief).

Handling relationship rejection

When an attempt to form a relationship is not reciprocated, we are left feeling disappointed or vulnerable, and we may feel helpless, resentful or even vengeful. In such situations, we need to understand our feelings The best way to do so is to examine the 'characters' in play. In this way, we can take responsibility for our actions *and* reactions.

Scenarios: Relationship and rejection

1. Job Application:
Chris had been with the same firm for fifteen years in a position of relatively high responsibility. He had received consistently excellent reviews and even financial bonuses. He was shocked when his company 'streamlined' production and he was made redundant. He enjoyed his work and unemployment came like a bolt from the blue.

After a period of recovery from the sudden change in circumstances, Chris applied for a number of jobs without success. He finally succeeded in being shortlisted.

The feedback from his interviews indicated he was a strong contender for the position and awaited the decision with high hopes. A week later he received a telephone call informing him that unfortunately his application had not been successful. Chris, having put so much effort mentally, emotionally and physically into obtaining the job, was not resilient enough to accept this rejection and became severely depressed.

This scenario demonstrates a shift from Chief (Chris in his former job) to Slave (when he is fired) to Warrior/Servant looking for a job and promoting himself in an interview to Slave (rejected).

2. Deep Personal Rejection:
Philip had been dating Joy for six months and, certain she was the right one for him, decided to propose.

He carefully planned this special occasion, reserving a table at an expensive restaurant and arranging to have her favourite flowers on the table and romantic music played. After coffee was served, Philip surprised Joy by proposing and was astounded when she turned him down flat.

Humiliated, Philip responded angrily: "After all my time and expense, I deserve better – not a kick in the teeth! You'll be sorry because if I can't have you no one will!"

This scenario demonstrates a shift from Warrior/Servant (trying to get the girl) to Servant/Warrior (planning the evening) to Warrior (his anger at rejection).

3. Rejection and recovery:

Hunter's girlfriend Becky closed the door quietly as she left the room, forever. At first he felt despondent, but then decided to move on. The following night he went to a local club.

Soon, one woman caught his eye and smiled at him. He went over and introduced himself and initiated a conversation.

Janice enjoyed the chat and sarcastically said, 'What else can you do?' 'I can dance, can you?' he responded sharply. 'Yes I can!' she shot back.

Hunter and Janice discovered that each of them enjoyed Latin American dancing. As they talked and danced, they discovered they had a lot in common, and decided to continue seeing each other.

This scenario demonstrates a shift from Slave (Hunter is rejected by Becky) to Warrior/Servant (he moves on) to Servant/Warrior (meeting Janice and discovering common ground).

Reasons we choose the Tribes to which we belong

Some people find joining groups intimidating, while others find the process challenging. It is the prospect of the unknown that can cause either fear of disappointment or excitement. Rejection may cause us to feel resentful or depressed, or it may allow us to move on to something else. Admittance to a group may produce a sense of relief and gratification. It does not automatically bring acceptance. As a new member of a group we can experience feelings of uncertainty because the unknown challenges our skills, our sense of identity. This can spill over into our relationships with others outside the group and to our personal values and can necessitate an evaluation of our own self-interest against that of the group.

When we join a group, we must consider not only the designated 'character' roles people play in the hierarchy of the group, but also the subtle expression of the 'characters' of the members in a social context. This often does not correspond to their official roles.

When we recognise the way the group's tribal hierarchy is structured and the contradiction between official and social roles, which are a source of conflict, then we can determine whether we are able or willing to adapt to the group culture. If we know our 'characters' and how they affect the roles we play, we may become a more successful member.

A person's 'character' type influences the groups they join. For instance a Servant type may be drawn to an autocratic, organised group. If we display a Warrior type we will want a more democratic structure. Chief types are often attracted to groups with inadequate management. Tribal culture and a person's 'character' type will influence the decision whether to join the group or not. Most of us will join a group to see if it fits with our personality. *(We may join a group to change our 'character' type.)*

At its best, a tribe works co-operatively so all members can get along and feel valued irrespective of the 'character' role they play. Emotional connection with others encourages a willingness to participate and contribute to the well-being of a group. Conversely, divisions can occur when only some members dominate and benefit. The lack of connection weakens and alienates our sense of obligation and our emotional identity with the group.

There are many reasons for joining or not joining a tribe, some of which are set out below. The following list might help you to discover what motivates you.

Reasons for wanting to join a tribe could include:	Reasons for not wanting to join a tribe could include:
➢ to gain more education, or to explore and extend our creativity	➢ fear of rejection
➢ to gain a sense of security through emotional connection	➢ feeling shy and/or unworthy
	➢ class and/or cultural prejudice
	➢ fear of intimacy or of not fitting in
➢ to avoid being alone	➢ fear of loss of identity
➢ to gain pleasure, joy, contentment and satisfaction	➢ differences in values and/or change of status
➢ to share common interests	➢ feelings of hostility towards a member of the group
➢ to gain status by demonstrating skills and knowledge	➢ fear of being undervalued or exploited
➢ to fulfil ambitions or for networking	➢ distrust due to past experiences of abuse (emotional, mental, physical or financial)
➢ to exploit a relationship for selfish reasons	➢ feelings of inadequacy or inferiority (related to education, or other reasons)
➢ to extend and maintain influence	➢ fear of others' expectations or demands
➢ to join a friend or friends in the tribe	
➢ to enhance future prospects.	

Whatever the reasons we have for not wanting to belong to a tribe, we will be connected to a tribe or tribes through direct or indirect relationships. Some people become reclusive to avoid being in a tribe, but they still have to deal with their own inner tribe.

Why you might be invited into a tribe:

➤ having an entertaining personality

➤ having the ability to build up morale and social networks

➤ having high value and to disadvantage the tribe you were with

➤ possessing skills and knowledge or beneficial material resources

➤ having emotional connections (through family or friends)

➤ ability to stifle external and interenal dissent

➤ High status and/orprestige to increase trible power

➤ As an humanitarian act to give protection and comfort

➤ To mediate between warring factions within the tribe

➤ to advantage or disadvantage, marginalise and/or displace individuals within the tribe

When we join a tribe, the intent can be:

➤ to gain resources and establish status – **Warrior**

➤ to enhance prestige – **Chief**

➤ to feel secure and valued – **Servant**

➤ to provide support and facilitate the development of ethical behaviour – **Mentor**.

Issues we may face when joining a group:

➤ adapting to change and modifying values

➤ accommodating various personality values and social differences

➤ the potential for strong emotional conflict to occur in the early days of the relationship (values conflict)

➤ changes in status, authority and credibility

Maintaining the tribal harmony

The roles people play has a value in keeping society in a state of harmony. They need to feel rewarded for their contribution. Feeling unappreciated for effort made is a recipe for conflict. For societies to survive and thrive it is necessary for individuals to feel their roles are important, whether they have a high or low status. A balanced distribution of assets, where the margin between the top echelons – Chiefs – and lower ranks – Warriors and Servants – are not too large will sustain a viable cultural structure. A tribe managed by an individual acting from her or his Primitive Chief will accumulate assets to meet the need to show power. There are many instances with this type of leader has used society's treasury as their own personal bank. When society's assets are understood to be hoarded by the higher ranks – Chiefs – the result is a decline in values and obligations within the tribe. When members of the tribe lose a sense of synergy, of obligation to each other, they have moved to a Warrior society where exploitation, pillage and plunder will prevail. A tribal society depends on individuals acting out the roles of Chiefs, Warriors, and Servants in synergy, and Mentors are required to achieve civil and social stability. From the top level of the tribe to the low levels the roles people play must be rewarded to ensure their continued contribution to the maintenance of tribal interests.

The qualities of the Servant in synergy with the other 'characters', and of the Mentor are crucial in maintaining tribal harmony. The heightened state of self-awareness of the Mentor in people shows they have an ability to see the prejudices and motivations in the tribal 'characters' in themselves and others by perceiving their strengths and weaknesses and by interpreting their varying perspectives. What could therefore help us understand the complex reality of a situation without prejudice or judgment so that we can respond from a humanitarian perspective beyond self and our tribe. When people express their Mentor they show empathy and compassion and care deeply about the broader community. This state, in conjunction with the Servant's need for emotional attachment, is a restraining force: *within an individual's personality* a contrast with our primitive impulses found in our Chief and Warrior. We seldom confront someone who possesses the black-and-white characteristics of the Warrior and the Chief. When we do, it is often in situations of tension and confrontation. The Servant and Mentor give our personalities light and shade. The Slave is not classified as a principal 'character'; being a Slave is a sub-state of the Servant and has no social standing. When we experience this state we feel unappreciated, powerless, or excluded.

It should be emphasized that *all* our 'characters' are motivated mainly by an unconscious desire for security; our primary purpose is to survive and to gain satisfaction. In society, the Warrior seeks to attain security by acquiring assets and status. The Chief seeks security by maintaining territory and power and the Servant seeks security by forming an emotional attachment. The Mentor seeks security by promoting a peaceful resolution to discord. The 'characters' relate to our collective co-existence, irrespective of whether we understand them or not. When all these security needs are met we gain validation in our relationship to others and society.

Tribal prejudices

Historically, prejudice was an important factor in a hostile environment. The tribe's practice of prejudice assured that members would abide by the law and customs of the tribe. Membership criteria were often based on blood ties, on defensive alliances against a common enemy or affiliation through trade. So

147

the history of tribal groups is steeped in bias that served to preserve cultural norms or alliances. People who voiced a different point view to the consensus view were a threat to the integrity of the tribe and would be put down forcefully. Five ideological principles governed the way in which tribes managed their culture: religion – as it is written; Royal edict; Tradition – what is handed down; Custom – common practices; patriarchal power – a male-dominated society. All these restricted any major deviation from tribal norms.

Though we live in a different time, the ingredients that make up a tribal or group structure still carry forms of prejudice. When we join groups there are many reasons for our choices. One major reason is our interest in forging a relationship with people who have similar interests, whereby we derive a sense of belonging and fellowship. We may join to contribute to the wider community, whether social or charitable. Membership could also be a way of promoting our own prejudices. A great deal depends on the tribe's cultural makeup, such as the limits of its boundary and philosophical flexibility that will determine the level of prejudice in the group.

When we join a group we have to be prepared to give up some of our independence in order to gain acceptance into the group. Surrendering autonomy plays a major role in shaping group culture, the basis on which individuals agree with the conditions that will defend the interests of the tribe and its structure. Tribal groups are formed from specific agendas. They are prone to exhibit prejudices against those they feel do not measure up to their standard or philosophy. When we join or are part of a group, we will share the same goals and ideologies, as well as conforming to group norms, to sustain an identity with the group.

Many societies have laws against discrimination. Despite such good intentions, discrimination still persists, for instance in stereotyping, or displaying favouritism towards one's own group, to people of a certain physical appearance and in consideration of a person's social and economic situation, whether rich or poor. Bias is also reflected in attitudes that prevent qualified people gaining employment or reaching top-level positions because of their ethnicity or gender. Then there are tribal political institutions that can be a breeding ground for prejudice, as found in political parties. This type of political bias is expressed by the Primitive Chief. There is no compromise: things are viewed from an ideological frame of reference, producing an intolerant culture. The Chief/Servant will be even-handed, showing compromise when differences appear in order to maintain the integrity of the group. That encourages tolerance within the group. The same is also true for individuals. The Primitive 'characters' will be dominant wherever there is an interest in protecting or advancing one's own opinions at the expense of others.

Prejudice can thrive in conflict and crisis situations, in which some individuals express the opportunistic nature of their Primitives to gain advantage. They will often use emotive language to stir up a feeling of being threatened to tie others to their point of view. They strengthen their power through ideological rhetoric, by instilling fear. These individuals play on the fears and insecurity of the Servant nature in others to produce a situation where they surrender their power. Propaganda is used to cause fear, switching people's civil responses to aggression because of the perception that they are under imminent threat. This type of fear is often employed to stimulate the prejudices found in the Primitive nature. The reaction can be seen in rampage and riots, and attacks on others who are supposedly a threat to their beliefs and physical interests. Those who are attacked are often considered to be inferior to the attackers.

Our tribal nature can cause us to reject information that is not in keeping with our cultural view of the world. That is why it is difficult to gain consensus when dealing with issues where strong cultural structures are in place. Such structures fog reality and make it difficult to gain trust.

Scenario: Blind prejudice

> James was promoted and he moved to a new location to work. After settling in he joined a social club similar to one to which he had previously belonged. Three months after joining, elections were to be held for club officers. He put his name forward for the position of Recruitment Officer, which he gained. In committee meetings he was enthusiastic about making changes that would bring in new members to offset their dwindling membership. James mentioned the changes his last club had put into practice to gain membership that had produced good results. He proposed that if it worked for his last club then it would work for this club. The proposal did not go down well with established members because they thought it would alter the whole culture of the club.

There are two forces of prejudice at work in this situation 1.) Established members expressing strong Chief to maintain culture and territory they identified 2.) James referencing his previous clubs' program suggested it was superior. James' Warrior wanted to bring into the club changes that would establish a culture that he could identify with and gave him status. The Mentor would have approached things in a reassuring way by building confidence in the process for change.

It is our Mentor who, when fully developed, gives us a greater sense of self. This means that we are able to see all our 'characters' and their prejudices in the context of any given situation; we are able to observe ourselves and others in a more perceptive way.

Conflict cycles

A conflict cycle entails a set of highly charged emotional responses. It often manifests in a one-sided co-dependency relationship that is emotionally destructive and/or abusive. It can evolve between family members, siblings, friends, or co-workers. When individuals play particular 'characters' from a rigid and vulnerable position and have no flexibility to accommodate change, they usually involve the Primitive Chief, the Persecutor, Slave – a persecuted avoider and the Warrior/Servant – a defending challenger. A conflict can leave the participants with underlying grievances, which sets the stage for future confrontations. Conflict can be terminated by any one or more of the participants withdrawing or having a willingness to accept someone outside the conflict as a mediator (Mentor).

Conflicts occur for multiple reasons, often related to an underlying grievance about others use of power or to gain revenge for injustices. Conflicts can also be a vent for past hurts that are totally unrelated to the present circumstances. It is only when individuals in conflict can see they are hurting others that they accept a responsibility to find a reasonable negotiated outcome. In emotionally charged situations there can often be confusion as to what really occurred because the issue is clouded by personal agendas. Underlying grievances and past hurt can amplify feelings, distorting perceptions and causing over-reaction: either aggression by the Primitives or submission by the Slave.

A recycling of past hurts can set up a conflict cycle. A cycle can often start with defensiveness developing into unreasonableness, expressed by the Primitives. The issue is unlikely to be resolved while these 'characters' are dominant. The Mentor expresses unprejudiced reasoning in conflict, suggesting time out or a tactful withdrawal by both sides. At that point the participants have taken the first steps to breaking the cycle.

In relationships where there is a close intertwining of activities, for example in families, workplaces (including in the home) and sports activities, patterns of stressful behaviour may occur. This may unconsciously trigger a predictable 'character' response, which can produce a conflict cycle where there are no disinterested parties to break a patterned response. You may have observed this happening in yourself, your own family, in other families, your workplace or club. Have you ever noticed that in these interactions people may show the same 'characters' in a drama, even though the issues may be different? Some individuals switch to particular 'characters', which makes it difficult for them to see other points of view, as occurs when an individual is able to stand back and become aware of their feelings. This gives them the opportunity to see the roles they take in a conflict, relinquish the need to triumph and act for the good of all concerned.

Past hurts and feelings of inadequacy can have a profound effect on the way a person uses power in a situation in which they are in managing or leadership roles. These stored feelings of hurt and inadequacy may find an outlet through their Primitives giving vent to these feelings by dominating or raging behaviour. They may even create conflict in order to vent feelings. This behaviour can produce confrontations, fear or recalcitrance in those for whom they have a responsibility of care; or they may be socially excluded by others as a way of limiting their insensitive behaviour.

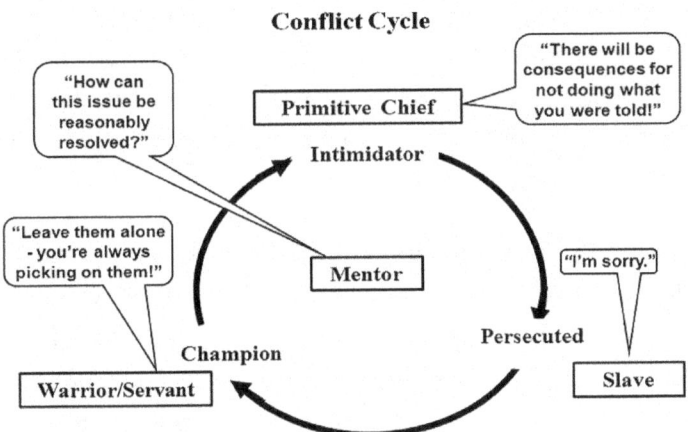

The Chief (Persecutor) asserts control by initiating the transaction and various 'characters' react to the Chief's demands. 'You have broken the rules!'

The subordinated individual is threatened (Persecuted – Slave). 'Why does it always happen to me?'

The Warrior/Servant (Defender) challenges the Chief in defence of the Slave. 'They don't deserve to be treated that way!'

The Mentor (Mediator) attempts to break the cycle by negotiating a solution. 'I can see there are a lot of hurt feelings.' Asking the question what action could be taken to resolve the issue amicably?

The Primitive Warrior may respond instead of the Slave by addressing the threat, 'To hell with you!' then leave the scene. This leaves the conflict to be restarted another time.

Sometimes we are faced with difficult situations and may instinctively respond from a specific 'character'. We may avoid conflict by being conciliatory, whereas others may be more inclined to confrontation and will not tolerate any domination. The circumstances of a given situation, combined with the strengths and weaknesses of our own 'characters', will determine how we respond. If a person expressing the Warrior/Servant in a particular conflict situation is accused of interfering, they might retreat to the feeling of the Slave or they might express their Warrior and attack the persecutor. Some of the issues underlying these cyclical events are low self-esteem, reactivity, poor communication, controlling behaviour, dependency, denial and problems with intimacy.

If anyone involved in the conflict cycle attempts to intervene with their Mentor, an opportunity to resolve the issue may emerge. However, the Mentor will have very little influence if tension is high. The tension must be somewhat reduced for the Mentor to have any effect on resolving the issue. Stepping into a conflict situation as a Mentor will be effective only if one or more of the others involved are willing to listen by stepping back from their Primitives. If the Mentor's mediation is effective, the conflict may be resolved without anger, emotional hurt or physical injury.

Issues that can develop a cyclical theme

Scenario: Addiction

> Peter has been drinking heavily all night. When he comes out of the bar, he asks belligerently, 'What stupid idiot has taken my car keys?' Philip responds, 'I've taken them, mate – I think you've had too much to drink!' Peter replies aggressively 'Who gave you the right to take my keys? Keep your nose out of my business!'
>
> Philip responds, 'I'm sorry,' and reluctantly hands the keys over. He then says, 'I'm really concerned for your safety, and that of other people. I'll take you home and we can come back for the car tomorrow!' Peter hands over the keys.

People with addictive behaviours are prone to conflict cycles. Peter responds from his Chief and demands his keys. Philip responds from his Servant/Warrior and appeals to his friend's common sense. Peter again responds from his Chief and demands his keys. Philip then responds from his Servant and reluctantly hands them over. His Mentor then offers Peter an option, in an attempt to avert a possible tragedy.

Conflict cycles can become internalised when in their internal dialogue a person becomes her or his own persecutor, victim and defender.

Scenarie: External conflict

> Barry's ten-year-old son runs into the living room in muddy shoes.
>
> Barry angrily shouts 'Get those dirty shoes out of here!'
>
> His son dejectedly replies 'I'm sorry, Dad.'
>
> Barry's wife Mary responds 'Why are you shouting at him like that?'
>
> Barry turns on Mary: 'He should know better! He does it all the time, and you never do anything about it!'
>
> Their son now responds, 'Don't yell at Mum!'
>
> Mary says, 'Son, take your shoes outside, please. And Barry, don't you think you are overreacting?'
>
> Barry responds, 'I did overreact – I shouldn't have shouted.'

The above situation illustrates the kind of situation that can develop into a recurring response to family issues.

Barry (Chief) reprimands his son. His son says he is sorry (Slave).

Mary (Warrior/Servant) defends their son, and criticises her husband (Chief).

Barry becomes more aggressive (Chief). Son (Chief) rebukes his father.

Mary attempts peace (Mentor). Barry (Mentor) acknowledges his error.

Scenario: Internal conflict dialogue

> Jackie is reversing her car out of her garage when she hears a loud crunch and realises she has hit something. When she checks she finds she has badly damaged her new water-blaster that had been left in the driveway.

You will note in the internal dialogue the words used which indicate the 'character' position related to the self. From this comes the possible internal responses from her own 'characters',

- *'That was a stupid thing to do! You didn't check to see if the driveway was clear! It's all your fault!' (internal Primitive Chief – condemnation).*
- *'Another one of those days – I can never do anything right!' (Infantile*
  Slave – self persecuting).
- *'This wouldn't have happened if John had put the bloody thing away!'*
  (Warrior/Servant – Defender).
- *'Accidents happen. I'll check the driveway in the future.' (Mentor -*
  Mediator).

A person can move from one Character role to another – internally or externally. She or he might act first as a tyrant, as with Barry towards his son or Jackie first admonishing herself. Reflection on their initial response allowed Barry and Jackie to shift to 'characters' that adopt a more conciliatory approach. The dynamics between our 'characters' are always shifting. How we respond to our own 'characters' and those of others depends largely on the predisposition of our nature. Sometimes we might surprise ourselves and respond in an unexpected manner – but often people follow their dominant 'character' type. It is when we become aware of the way 'characters' influence our lives that we have choices in breaking conflict cycles.

Shifting 'characters' is very common. An individual may move from being a friend to becoming an adversary, victim, or rescuer.

Scenario: Scene-shifting

> Freda, Joanne and Pete are having an amicable discussion when Joanne says something to Freda that offends her. Freda accuses Joanne of being insensitive and Joanne bursts into tears. Pete then criticises Freda for overreacting and for her antagonistic attitude towards Joanne. Instead of apologising for her inappropriate behaviour Freda responds by accusing Pete of making things worse by interfering when it is none of his business. Joanne then steps in saying, 'I don't want to deal with this anymore. Stop it!'

In theatrical terms this behaviour is called scene-shifting – keeping the drama fresh by giving it a sense of unpredictability. But this kind of shifting of 'characters' occurs in real life too – one person who changes seemingly without provocation from one role to another. When Freda is offended she responds from her Warrior to both Joanne and Pete. Pete behaves as Chief when he criticises Freda, which does not alleviate the situation. Joanne having responded from the Slave switches to Chief commanding a stop to the conversation.

158

Addictive behaviour

Addiction has become a major issue in society. Let's look at what addictions are and at the 'characters' that perpetuate the problem. Addiction lurks within us all; addictive impulses can take over our lives, diminishing any sense of self. Addictive behaviour is derived from a number of emotional sources: powerlessness, anxiety and uncertainty produce fear and threats to safety, stimulating the action of the Primitive Warrior. There is an instinctive hunger to soothe these feelings that is so powerful that it divorces us from reality. It affects self-control and self-preservation. Until an individual has gained some degree of 'character' synergy, particularly Chief/Servant synergy, the capability to control emotional impulses and to focus or shift attention is limited. Without this synergy an individual is less able to distract herself or himself from unpleasant feelings or overcome strong impulses, resulting in distress.

The Servant and Mentor in synergy educates the Warrior and Chief, taming our Primitive nature. This internal consensus to act in a cooperative way decreases the likelihood of addiction. It can help to form strategies to counter tendencies toward re-addiction. The 'character' that can change addictive behaviour is the Chief/Servant, a synergy that focuses on self-responsibility in managing behaviour in a person's life. The Servant/Warrior helps to build emotional connection and the Mentor to find wisdom from experience. These develop socially competent and self-assured individuals.

If, in childhood, there is insufficient 'character' synergy the child will be vulnerable to her or his emotions and unable to develop moral boundaries to restrain impulsive feelings. This lack of social structure can be experienced as anxiety arising from a lack of self-confidence, poor self-discipline, or an

159

inability to exercise deferred gratification. When 'character' synergy starts to form in a person it helps them develop impulse control. Impulse control evaluates feelings and intentions and possible consequence on others as well as oneself. Helping our children to develop 'character' synergy assists them to avoid addictive behaviour restrains forming the instinctive urges found in the Primitive Characters into civilised expressions. If children are encouraged to be respectful, to take responsibility for their actions and to learn the importance of service to others, they have a greater chance to develop the attributes found in the Chief/Servant and Servant/Warrior synergy, which are necessary for self-control and honouring obligations and building emotional connection that gives a sense of self and allows them to identify with others. Research suggests there is a genetic component to some people being prone to addictive behaviour. That does not mean people with this disposition are incapable of developing 'character synergy'. What is needed is to help them to develop the attributes of the 'characters' necessary for self-control.

The phases of addiction

There are two phases in addiction. The first is the addictive phase, where the only goal is to satisfy the hunger to subdue the anxieties felt and in which there is little or no remorse for the actions of the addict. The second is the rehabilitation phase, which is experienced as feelings of failure, guilt, blaming, and anguish, which surface from the Infantile Slave. At the lowest level of this phase of powerlessness the cycle may lead back to the addictive phase in order to relieve the feelings found in the Infantile Slave's emotional pain.

It is often difficult for those who are emotionally attached to addicts to help them, particularly parents and friends, who tend to express their Servant/Chief and act as a rescuer. This 'character' synergy is highly emotionally sensitive, which colours judgment, leaving the would-be rescuer vulnerable to manipulation and unintentionally aiding and abetting the addict. Empathy can turn to feelings of powerlessness as the Infantile Slave watches the decline of the addict, or abandons him or her. Individuals responding from the Chief/Servant synergy will be clear thinking as well as empathetic. They will offer a practical approach to rehabilitation with the aim of helping the addict change his or her behaviour. They see the reality of the situation, aware of manipulative behaviour by a person with a lack of impulse control. They also see the need for the addict, with some support, to take personal responsibility for helping himself or herself.

As previously stated, the Primitive Warrior in the developing child is the instinctive nature that is necessary for biological survival. This instinctive nature can be civilised by social conditioning. In the acquisitive pressures of today's society, our Primitive Warrior is more inclined to find expression. Adolescence is a particularly vulnerable time for the potential to develop addictions. It is a time where the societal restraints of cultural norms and values may be eroded or totally cast aside for 'freedom.' This rebellious adolescent attitude unwittingly adds to the sense of internal insecurity. Although addictive behaviour can develop at any time in the life cycle, adolescence is the most critical time for anti-social and addictive behaviours to develop.

Addiction can develop in the Chief and Servant. In the Chief it may stem from feelings of inadequacy, characterised by fear, expressed in an unreasonable desire to maintain power and control regardless of the consequences to others. In the Servant, addiction springs from the fear of disapproval and rejection, and is characterised by an obsessive need to please, ending up in Slave behaviour.

Acquisitiveness

The acquisitive nature of society encourages addiction. We live in a culture which emphasizes consumption over conservation – it is the latter which creates the frameworks that maintain and build a healthy society (and therefore exercise a form of restraint on our primitive behaviour).

Our acquisitiveness is reflected in nearly every aspect of life. We are consuming far more than we need. There is little or no structure to tribal culture, e.g., traditions, customs, parental control, that promotes restraint.

When we acquire without obligation we are open to developing excesses that are found in the Primitive Warrior. It is only when we develop a sense of ownership (Chief/Servant) and obligation (Servant) that we can gain a sense of connection and mutual respect for other individuals also linked to our tribe. A lack of connection leaves us vulnerable to destructive behaviours that are isolating – which is a key component of addiction.

'Feminine' and 'masculine' qualities expressed by the 'characters'

Until the last 60 years the roles people have played in the hierarchy of social structures in Western societies were influenced by gender. Males acted from their Chief and Warrior 'characters', which gave them controlling roles over family and assets. Society expected females to be submissive. They were required to act from their Servant and could be also be relegated to become Slaves.

This culturally constructed behaviour was the norm until the beginning of the twentieth century, when things started to change. In western society today, both men and women are free to develop all their 'characters'. This means that the 'characters' are no longer determined by gender, making relationships more complicated and sophisticated, and we have to work harder to create balance. The tribal model works within a 'genderless' framework. The model is nature's design in which the roles were not specifically assigned to one gender.

Rather than examining behaviours in terms of traditional male-female roles, we are interested in looking at behaviour rules governing the 'characters' we play that are non-gender specific – women can be Chief/Servant or Warrior/Servant as much as men can, and men can be nurturing, as expressed by the Servant/Chief. There is no 'character' trait exclusive to any one gender. We are all made up of both 'masculine' and 'feminine' attributes. The 'characters' drive an individual's personality, and both men and women possess within them all the 'character' traits, from the Primitives to the synergistic 'characters'.

The 'characters' influence our communication style, and that too is genderless. Whereas communication has commonly been described as 'feminine' and 'masculine' we mention here that the style we adopt is determined by our 'characters' more than anything else – including our gender. Clearly, there are *inclusive* and *exclusive* styles – but those, too, do not necessarily need to be characterised as feminine or masculine. The *roles* define people in terms of action rather than disposition – whereas characteristics have traditionally been defined in terms of their masculine or feminine qualities, we mean to show that these can be better defined in terms of response and action. Therefore we have specifically avoided talking in terms of 'male' or 'female' behaviours.

Individuals with 'empathetic' tendencies (those tendencies that may traditionally have been called 'feminine') express the Servant synergistic with other 'characters' (Servant/Chief and

163

Servant/Warrior). They tend toward openness and are generally congenial, and strive to build communication and intimacy to accomplish social connection. They form friendships based on mutual support.

Common 'empathetic' tendencies (popularly perceived as 'feminine' traits):

- Nurturing
- Sympathetic
- Patient
- Dependent
- Congenial
- Cooperative
- Sensitive
- Intuitive
- Receptive
- Cautious
- Emotional
- Trusting

'Controlling' tendencies (those tendencies which might traditionally have been called 'masculine') are found in the Chief/Servant and Warrior/Servant. Both these synergies avoid portraying weakness and vulnerability. They are less emotionally sensitive, they see things from a more mental, analytical perspective. They form relationships that give some form of mental or physical return.

Common 'controlling' tendencies (popularly perceived 'masculine' traits):

- Dominant
- Independent minded
- Ambitious
- Status-seeking
- Aggression
- Political
- Tough
- Iinsensitive
- Rational
- Analytical
- Competitive
- Sexually assertive

As we have said previously in this work, 'character' does not define gender. Each individual holds feminine and masculine attributes within her or his nature. What we're showing is that in any individual there is a tendency to express specific 'characters', whether their behaviour is in the feminine or masculine spectrum.

Tribal arguments and battles

Where there is a dispute between two or more people, the 'characters' they express will hold a particular position, which will in turn either exacerbate or reduce tension. An examination of the 'characters' used by the people on either side of an issue will tell us whether the dispute can or cannot be resolved. We can gain an understanding why people turn out to be either peaceful or in a state of continuous strife. In most conflict situations there is usually high tension and strong emotion displayed. It can be difficult for people to stop themselves from further damaging a relationship. So it is important that we understand the kind of atmosphere we promote by the 'characters' we use in dealing with such situations. If we respond from our Primitive Warrior we will further inflame the situation and violence could easily result. Responding from our Primitive Chief, we hold stubbornly to our position but would end hostilities if we thought the other person had backed down. When we engage the Mentor we can find reason and an ethical outcome. So when we examine conflicts we have to consider the context leading up to the problem and the 'characters' in play. By examining the 'characters' in the conflict you will get a better idea of what is at stake if the problem escalates. Knowing the characters involved can lead to the development of a mutually consensual approach in conflict situations.

Things that spark a conflict are often not the real issue. The real issue is the individual or group 'character' types. The 'characters' used are often those that connect the individual to some past issue; or an individual sees the present situation as a threat. Defining what causes the conflict and the 'characters' used in any given situation will lead to a more constructive approach when conflict occurs. Then we can understand why people– individuals, families, communities, even nations – fall out.

The terms 'hot war', 'cold war' and 'rebellion' illustrate different types of conflicts. A 'hot war' is expressed by the Primitive Warrior: conflict is of a physical, violent nature, from both sides. It is a state of open warfare and involves verbal abuse and physical violence on both sides. It is a 'win at any cost' response with no regard for the effect on innocent parties such as children or other bystanders.

A 'cold war' is a conflict between individuals expressing their Primitive Chief, whose main goal is to undermine the other's position. It most often produces a 'standoff', a state of undeclared hostility, and involves defensive dialogue and posturing. It is accompanied by a refusal to negotiate, as in: 'You can do what you like, but I'm not changing!' 'Rebellion' occurs when a person reacts from their Primitive Warrior to feelings of being dominated by others who are acting from their Primitive Chief. It is a protest or a refusal to accept the demands or conditions imposed. It is seen when a person feels their skills are not being appropriately rewarded or that they are undervalued or being treated like a Slave. The person's Primitive Warrior seeks revenge by verbally or physically attacking those the person feels have imposed these painful conditions.

Different types of conflict

Civil war is a war between organised groups within the same nation state. The phrase can be applied to families or groups. It is hostile opposing views within a relationship that break out into conflict; fights over inheritances; interdepartmental conflict within a corporation or membership against the administration within a club.

Incursion – entering another's territory (room or dwelling) **example:** an intentional invasion of someone's space knowing it would offend or intimidate.

Intimidation – frightening others into respecting your power. You feel you have to encourage them to comply with your demands. Aggressive partner or boss.

Obstruction – delaying tactics, hiding damaging information, stalling in order gain advantage

Silence – attitude which ignores and excludes, for example a 'cold shoulder'; giving off 'vibes' in order to cause discomfort or indicate disapproval.

Skirmish – a minor dispute, short-lived, example: petty quarrel; sibling rivalry.

These disputes often involve territorial issues in which people see their opponents as infringing their rights; or they consider themselves equals in a bid to win dominance and greater status, seeking to weaken others. Either party, while expressing their Chief, may shift to the Warrior. If this happens the conflict will escalate, and the result will be a change from cold war to a hot war.

Additionally, an individual may act on their Recalcitrant Slave (which is a sub-state of the Primitive Warrior) and engage in subterfuge, withholding information, giving out deceptive information, spreading rumours and innuendoes (partial truths or untruths), etc. When people experience either the Primitive Warrior or Recalcitrant Slave the feelings in both states are the same, though people will act differently. When an individual feels undervalued and excluded, the resulting resentment and feelings of rage can build and contribute to an outburst of the Primitive Warrior or to resentments that will be held in the Recalcitrant Slave.

Scenario: Three stages of conflict

Rebecca and John decide to live together and agree they will share the household tasks. Things work well for the first few months; however, Rebecca soon finds herself constantly reminding John to complete his share of the tasks.

Frustrated, Rebecca confronts John about his lack of commitment. His response is, 'I do enough around here.'

Rebecca shoots back, 'You've got plenty of time – you only work part time anyway!' and then she adds, 'If you're not going to contribute, neither will I!' John replies, 'If you'd stop your nagging it would help! I won't change until *you* change!' Both stubbornly stick to their stated positions.

Rebecca goes outside to bring in the washing and John follows. Rebecca takes the washing off the line and throws it blindly towards the laundry basket with some of the clothes falling on the ground. The conflict escalates. They scream at one another and Rebecca lunges at John. He grabs her, and they wrestle.

Rebecca feels like a Slave, used and unappreciated, and responds from her Warrior (rebellion) and aggressively confronts John. John reacts defensively from his Chief. Rebecca then responds from her Chief, which creates a standoff (cold war). The conflict then escalates at the laundry line - Warrior to Warrior (hot war).

As you see in this scenario, conflicts can apply to the personal as well as to the tribe or nation; the elements are the same. Recognizing these different kinds of conflicts and including the synergistic 'characters' or Mentor it will help us diffuse potential warlike situations.

Conflict resolution

Communication skills can provide us with powerful tools to reduce conflict if we explore the situation to determine if the conditions are suitable for conflict resolution. We can make enquiries to see if the individuals involved are able to resolve the problem by themselves, or if they need a mediator. What ever they decide, the question is whether the issue is a local one or whether it possesses a wider impact on others outside the immediate participants. Can the issue be kept apart from the rest of the relationship? If an issue is unable to be resolved at this time, can conflict be postponed until the issue can be dealt with in a more neutral atmosphere? Finally, how can any agreement be monitored so each party can be confident that it will be honoured?

In any conflict situation, individuals who feel wronged (emotionally or physically) assume a 'character' position. Additionally, the 'characters' we play in resolving the issue will also affect the outcome. If the Warrior dominates, the conflict will continue with aggressive outbursts. If the Chief dominates, a standoff will occur and hostilities will simmer. If either party still feels injured after an agreement has been reached, he or she will experience the feeling of the Slave. It is only when the Mentor is involved that a fruitful outcome can occur. Our Mentor helps us achieve a peaceful negotiation. In any conflict situation there needs to be a starting point, a truce in which both sides feel safe. Then, introduce the mediation process: "What is on the table to be discussed?" Each person needs to be prepared to give up some positions held to reach agreement. It is also important to point out which 'characters' are involved in a conflict situation and how to engage the Mentor through self-evaluation.

Peace is always fragile and impermanent. Even though we negotiate a peace through truce, mediation, bargaining or treaty, the peace may still be broken. Understanding the way our 'characters' interact can give us a way of withdrawing from conflicts and maintaining a better peace – and therefore improve our relationships.

Scenario: Managing conflict

Mike becomes upset at his supervisor's continual criticism of his department, for he considers the work in his department far above par. He soon learns that Henry, another member of staff, is experiencing a similar problem with the same person. He contacts Henry and suggests they jointly approach management.

Mike feels disadvantaged (Slave) but by discussing his situation with other people his confidence is restored (Servant/Warrior), which enables him to take action (Warrior/Servant).

Tribal organisational structures in governments and industry

Governments and industry all apply tribal hierarchical structures in their managing processes. In any organisation the tribal hierarchical structure prevails. The CEO is the Chief, controlling and delegating to achieve the aims of the organisation. The Warrrior; the external agent benefiting its growth. Then there is the Servant acting in the administration and distribution functions.

The pyramids of power The management structure is a natural way we manage societies from tribal societies to a nation, then Empire and Globalisation.

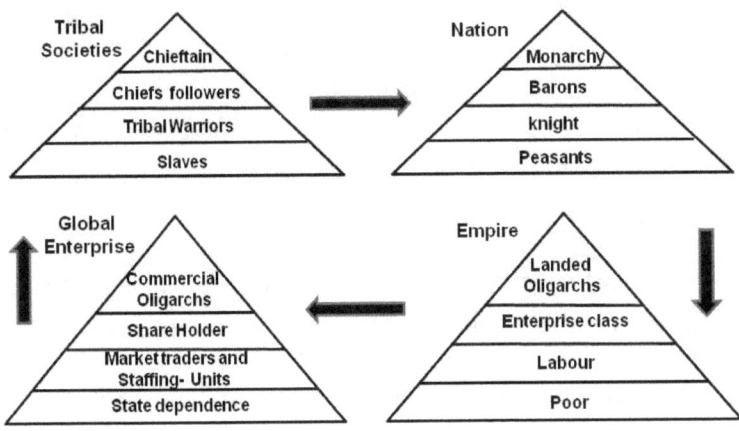

It is important that the organisation has a Chief/Servant type personality at the helm who is able to build rapport with the staff, thus reducing the likelihood that personal issues and resentment impinges on the organisation's culture. Honesty and consistency are essential to give reassurance and a sense of reliability. Honest and consistent leadership can be depended upon. In this atmosphere it is easier to create consensus and a shared vision.

Effective communication is a quality of this 'character' synergy that helps to keep the team working on the right track. People who express this personality type will be flexible to new ideas and open-minded enough to apply them on merit. The Mentor is important in the management of an organisation, giving the organisation the willingness to explore its own cultural biases

Administrative staff supply information, processing instructions to others within the organisation. These are Servant/Chief types who are responsible for maintaining the connective tissue of the organisation. Research and development is where you will find the Servant/Warrior types. Then there are the Warrior/Servant types, who are found in sales and marketing or resource gathering: they are entrepreneurial. Finally, the ancillary staff such as cleaners and maintenance people is the Slave class. This is because their function does not directly contribute to production and distribution. So you can see how the 'characters' define divisions of labour with an organisation. To re-state an earlier observation, the word 'Slave' is not used to denigrate but to illustrate the historical reference that is reflected today in the organisational ranking of labour.

Let's take you to a scenario to illustrate the role of 'characters' historically and to show how it is still relevant today.

If you were to find yourself in a besieged fortress, you would hope that there was a well organised and experienced Chief to arrange its defence and enough skilled Warriors to gain victory. You would also hope there were sufficient Servants to convey information between the chief and warriors and to distribute powder and shot. The wisdom of the Mentor would be essential to advise, guide, and negotiate peace so that a legacy of war is not left to the next generation.

The organisational structures are based on the tribal template. It defines roles and functions. It shows how everything fits together into a whole. When everyone in a tribe understands their tribal structure, they are better able to work together and perform their roles effectively.

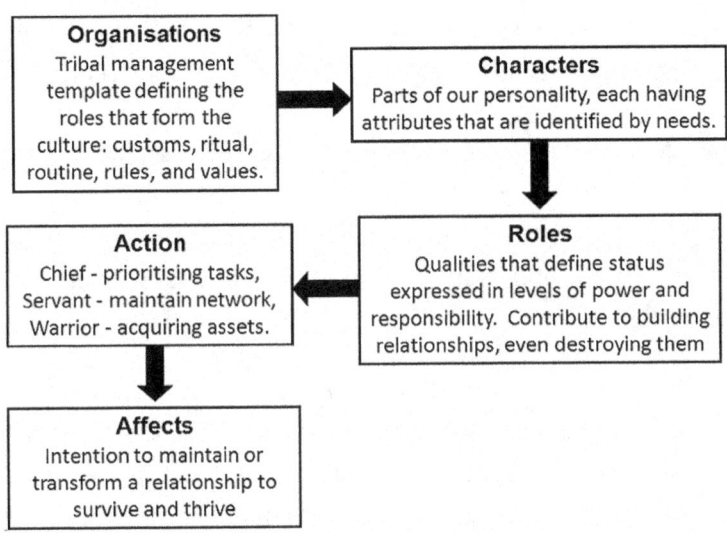

We have used this example to illustrate the historic formal roles in an organisational structure that apply today to any group. For instance the roles of Chiefs (CEO/Managers) are expected to show leadership to the Servant (clerical staff to intermediate staff between the different levels of the organisation) and Warriors (marketing/sales is the root of entrepreneurial activity) to gain what is needed to sustain the organisation. Mentors are advisers to provide help in time of crisis and controversy.

Civil Society

- (Chiefs) President, Prime Minister, ruling elite, military elite

Corporate Society

- (Chiefs) CEO and board of directors
- (Servants) Administrators,

- (Servants) Civil service, bureaucratic administrators, educators, members of the judiciary and police
- (Warriors) Business leaders, entrepreneurs
- (Slave) Labourers, artisans, the unemployed

- human resources, departmental heads, system administrators, secretaries
- (Warriors) Marketing/Sales
- (Slave) Ancillary staff and/or part time workers. individuals who maintain the physical structures

An organisation is an association of individuals with a common purpose. Within any organisation we find roles that define responsibilities to ensure the survival of that organisation. These roles represent a hierarchy, and that hierarchy is defined by rank and function.

Note that these organisational structures can be applied to both civil society and corporate frameworks. The Chief (executive leader or CEO) represents the executive level that authorises activities and sets objectives. The Servant (MPs and bureaucracy) link all the activities of the organisation. The Warrior class in private enterprises (entrepreneurs or marketing executives) pursue the goal of maximising capital and power. The Slaves maintain physical infrastructure, utilities, technical and other types of ancillary function.

Individuals in positions of responsibility who continually express their Primitive nature produce conflict and stress in relationships, which inevitably leads to resentment, disrupts work practices, produces lower quality work, lessens productivity and reduces a sense of mutual regard and commitment. The contrast we see in the above scenarios demonstrates the differences between the Primitive focus of self-interest and a more synergistic 'character' response that values teamwork and cooperation

It is important to understand how hierarchies work in an organisational framework *and* how individuals within that framework play out their 'character' roles. The roles we play influence organisational culture, both internally and externally, and impacts the success or failure of any organisation. Think of a stressful situation you have observed in a place where you have worked and of the 'characters' at play.

Scenario: Growing pains

Jeff has built his software company from the ground up. His easy-going personality makes him a personable boss, and his employees have always found him to be approachable. In recent months, the company has grown dynamically, and Jeff has hired a marketing team to help him envision a new direction. He recognizes the need to grow, but is overwhelmed by the speed with which change is occurring. He is increasingly short-tempered and demanding, and his employees notice that the rapport they have always felt has eroded.

In this scenario, Jeff begins as an admired business leader and becomes a benign and well-respected boss (Chief/Servant). He recognises the opportunity to grow and follows his ambition to make his company bigger and better (Warrior/Servant). The process, however, grows out of his control and he begins to feel powerless (Slave). The stress of the rapid changes gets to him and he lashes out at his staff (Primitive Chief).

Character profiles within an organisation

It is the people who matter in any organisation. Civil society rests with its participating members; corporate culture relies on the individuals who make companies work. Let us now review the types of personalities associated with each 'character' role in a group or organisation. Warrior/Servant types will seek to gain accolades for their achievements with the intention of gaining status. They are often found in the Marketing and Sales departments. Servant/Warrior types work diligently to gain bonds with the group, showing a team spirit. These types are a great asset in administration. Chief/Servant types, on the other hand, motivate, monitor and evaluate, encouraging others to cooperate. You would hope they are part of your top management team. Servant/Chief types build morale through supporting personal development and encouraging appreciation of the culture. These individuals are beneficial in the human resource area. Servant types carry out the job willingly without question, with a sense their interest is being looked after. They need to be encouraged to grow in the organisation.

The following 'character' types are damaging to any organisation. It is the only threat to the survival of the organisation where these 'characters' may be of value, but only in the most restrained expression of these 'characters'. Primitive Chief types are uncompromising. They see the organisation's interest as their own and will fight to the last to defend their interests. Primitive Warrior types are self-oriented. They will be totally ruthless in their efforts to gain what they want. Recalcitrant Slave types can and do bring down organisations by producing unexpected events.

Organisation of the military tribe

The military is the tribe within the tribe. Its function is to act in time of emergency to support the maintenance of order or to impose order. The military is the most powerful and efficient tribal organisation in society. It holds all the tribal assets, such as cherishing its history: battles won and lost, lessons learned, and giving homage to the fallen and the brave. The military also plans constantly for eventualities. It keeps firmly to its hierarchical structures. The tribal roles within the military are specifically defined so that each individual is responsible for the security and integrity of the tribe. When civil society falls apart the military is called on to impose its structure. This is the default structure on which civil society rebuilds from the chaos that causes the military to be called to re-establish order.

Today's Warrior society

In the past two and half centuries, there has been a decline in cultural values. Cultural values were vested in social institutions that held societies and nations together; religion, family, marriage, traditions and ethnic identity. This is not to say that these social institutions were good or bad. Their function was to maintain the synergistic behaviours of the 'characters' that were wrapped in customs and rituals, giving a socially recognised form of behaviour. These institutions gave a point of reference regarding standards, where people were expected to respect social codes of conduct. Today, people measure behaviour from a personal perspective that carries a self-interested bias.

These changes in society have given us greater freedoms to express ourselves and more independence than any generation before. But all this has not come without cost to our sense of belonging to a community that nurtures our sense of emotional connection. It is belonging to a tribe that sustains us in our mutual obligations to each other. These changes have also reduced the synergistic qualities of the roles we play that maintain the long-term integrity of a society.

If we compare the generations that lived before 1960 and those that followed, we will see several factors that set them apart. In earlier generations ordinary people experienced shortages of basic commodities. They were expected to manage their budget in a thrifty way. What this meant was to delay gratification, to wait until you could afford what you wanted. Children learned the adage that what they wanted was not what they would get. They learned that the household budget was for the necessities of life. It was a culture that required sacrifice and discipline. There were larger families and the older children learned to take responsibility for their siblings. There was a hierarchy of responsibility that built tribal values. It is true the elite class had greater freedom, but it too was restrained by social conventions. The 'sixties generation' ushered in a new benchmark for maturity, questioning social institutions. They abandoned historic parental values. It was an age of protest, and of questioning the accepted way of doing things. This was a time for overthrowing the old ways. There was a strong anti-authority feeling throughout this decade and it continues, not just with youth but also in the wider community. This can be seen in changes in social attitudes. The notion of obligation and loyalty has lost a great deal of meaning in today's society.

Our culture has emphasised consumerism. Children learn to be consumers at a very early age. As consumers they claim an interest in the household budget for their own self-interest. They are being given a sense of entitlement without the need to make a contribution, strengthening Primitive Warrior traits at a time they need to be encouraged to develop the synergistic 'character' traits. As they grow up they learn that sex is considered a recreational activity without commitment, and that one's physical image gains social status and a lack of self-discipline is an expression of individuality. The past is blamed for present inadequacies in order to excuse inappropriate behaviour. These standards of behaviour will leave future generations with a diminished sense of responsibility for maintaining tribal obligations. They will be Warriors without a tribe and without moral reference. The loss of parental values found in the tribal Chief/Servant qualities is leaving societies without cultural and social anchors.

To explain this further, the 'characters' in our nature contribute to social trends that influence the direction society takes. These movements are a response to social and environmental changes. If a particular 'character' becomes dominant, its traits will be reflected in society. For instance if the nature of the Chief is dominant in society, society will be autocratic and ideological in its make-up. Today we see a strong Warrior 'character' emphasis in people's attitudes. An indication of a Warrior Society is narcissism, which is encouraged by an individualistic mindset that is open to rapacious, exploitative and manipulative attitudes. These behaviours are driven by primal anxiety – fear of starvation – which is intensified by consumerism, creates a society with a lack of emotional connection to itself. This is seen in the lack of self-discipline, in addiction and self-indulgence. When Warrior traits are dominant there is a risk of social and moral decay. The more synergistic relationships between the 'characters', the more cooperative and inclusive the society. The question is whether we can change the path our societies are taking. Change is possible if we act from the qualities of the Chief/Servant and Servant/Chief in managing the interests of all the members of the global tribes. We will be maintaining the balance between our acquisitive nature and our social and environmental responsibilities. It is also important to have the Warrior/Servant present for renewal and a sense of advancement. Then, there is the Servant/Warrior nature, being prepared to draw our attention to social inadequacies.

We have all contributed in some way to society's unfolding problems. We believe there is a need to understand the way our tribal nature works in order to have a realistic view of the direction our world is taking. With such an understanding we can find answers to real social and environmental problems. We hope that this work has given a new perspective on the reasons we behave the way we do.

Glossary of Terms

Ambiguous dialogue: deceptive or *vagueness not saying exactly what is meant.*

Banter: teasing and joking, (*Which can graduate to more aggressive verbal duelling, perhaps with the intent of disarming or of humiliating).*

'Character' signature: behaviour that indicates the 'character's' identity.

'Character' synergy: the combining of the 'character' traits that form civil or social behaviour.

'Character' surrogates: person acting on behalf of another, thereby taking on their responsibilities.

Civilised communication: instructive and reasoned approach with the intent of achieving compliance.

Civilising the Chief: development of protocols, traditions and customs of leadership which serve group needs and civilises.

Conflicts within a tribe: personalities that inhibit effective and cooperative communication

Culture: traditional patterns, traits that incorporate beliefs, custom, speech and manners important to a tribe/society.

Dependency conditioning: feeling obligated to others.

Emotional connection: establishing a relationship to fulfil an emotional need.

Infantile anxiety: feeling, without any cognitive reference.

Infantile Slave: feeling fearful, powerless, being entrapped by circumstances and dependency.

Instinctive survival behaviour: uncompromising self-preservation.

Internal dialogues: mental self-talk between Tribal 'characters'.

Machiavellian: behaving in a crafty and deceitful manner to gain or maintain power.

Mentor: personal conscience.

Primary Tribal 'characters': Chief, Warrior and Servant – these have a direct influence on our physical and emotional survival.

Primitive: basic core nature – the instinctive survival behaviour.

Recalcitrant Slave: someone who is resentful and resistant to authority.

Relationship of convenience: devoid of emotional ties.

Role-specific relationships: assigning of roles that mark boundaries and behaviour within a relationship.

Slave: a person who feels subservient, treated as a chattel, of no account, no value.

Socialised communication: friendly and cooperative communication which fosters valuable and productive interactions within the tribe.

Socialising the Warrior: formation of emotional bonds and developing shared interests.

Socialising: process of establishing friendly relations which increase co-operation/intimacy.

Socialising: seeking out or enjoy the company of others.

Switching: moving from one 'character' to another with conscious or unconscious intent.

Traditions: patterns, behaviours and traits, passed down continuously from generation to generation.

Tribal 'character' communication: transactions between the 'characters' that produce specific responses, e.g. speech and intent.

Tribal 'characters': divisions of behaviour that make up our personalities.

Tribal emotional intelligence: ability to identify the 'characters'' emotional signatures and their influences on behaviour.

Tribal memory: collective consciousness/ancestral experience – containing values and beliefs inherited from childhood.

Tribalisation: Servant's influence on the behaviour of the Primitive 'characters' to strongly identity with and loyalty to one's tribe or group.

Tribalistic: having a strong feeling of identity and loyalty to one's tribe or group.

Tribe/Mentor: tribal conscience *(group responds compassionately to others outside their sphere of interest.*

Tribe: (i) individuals sharing customs held together by traditions that are handed down to each generation.

(ii) group or organisation – a network which relies on each individual playing their part to contribute to the common good.

(iii) oldest and most successful organisational model devised. Its main purpose is to produce a sense of social identity that strengthens the ability of the individual and the collective to survive. Tribal behaviour tends to be based on mutual defence, respect, and honour.